ENVISIONING DEMOCRACY

ENVISIONING DEMOCRACY:

The Role and Potential of Information and Communication Technologies for the Visually Impaired

Lloyd G. Waller

IAN RANDLE PUBLISHERS
Kingston • Miami

First published in Jamaica, 2017 by
Ian Randle Publishers
16 Herb McKenley Drive
Box 686
Kingston 6, Jamaica W.I.
www.ianrandlepublishers.com

© 2017 Lloyd G. Waller

ISBN: 978-976-637-947-6

National Library of Jamaica Cataloguing in Publication Data

Waller, Lloyd G.
  Envisioning democracy: the role and potential of information and
communication technologies for the visually impaired / Lloyd G. Waller.

    p. ; cm
Includes bibliographical references and index.
ISBN 978-976-637-947-6 (pbk)

1. Information technology – Political aspects
2. Information technology – Social aspects
3. People with visual disabilities – Political activity
4. Political participation – Technological innovations – Caribbean Area
I. Title

303.4833   dc 23

Cover photograph courtesy of Hugh Johnson
Cover graphics by Anya Gloudon
Cover and book design by Ian Randle Publishers
Printed and bound in the United States of America

*To my mother, Sybil Waller. For
her advice, patience and faith.
Because she always understood.*

Table of Contents

List of Figures & Tables

Preface and Acknowledgements

The exclusion of persons with disabilities (PWDs) from the social, economic, and political space of a country can be considered a human rights issue. Beyond that, being excluded from the participatory nexus of a country means that on the one hand, PWDs are unable to make a contribution to the growth and direction of that country; and on the other, a welfare burden is placed on that country as well. Exclusion, therefore, also becomes a development issue. Information Communication Technology (ICT) today enables and empowers PWDs to participate in the economic and social activities of a country. Though this is well recognized in the literature, not much research has been undertaken to explore how and in what ways ICTs contribute to the empowering and enabling PWDs to participate in the political activities of a country. The goal of this book therefore is to highlight and draw attention to the experiences of visually impaired persons with the use of ICTs to access the democratic space in Jamaica and Barbados.

ICTs are slowly becoming cheaper and more accessible in many parts of the world. Additionally, and, specifically as it relates to persons with disabilities, an increasing number of software and hardware manufacturers are embedding accessibility functions, which make these technologies easy to use. For example, several Apple products, particularly the iPhone and the iPad, have several features to help the visually impaired to interact and engage with objects, subjects, structures and systems as well as participate in events and processes. These features include VoiceOver, Zoom, Invert Colors, Grayscale, Speech: Speak Selection, Speak Screen, Speak Auto-text, Larger Text, Bold Text, Button Shapes, Increase Contrast, Reduce Motion and On/Off Labels. Similarly, Microsoft, another software giant, has built in several accessibility functions in its popular Windows operating system which is also of value to the visually impaired. In Windows 10, for example, new features include hearing text read aloud with Narrator, magnifier, the of use text or visual alternative to sounds, the use of the On-Screen Keyboard (OSK) to type as well as Speech Recognition to control the computer and allow someone who is visually impaired to operate a computer or mobile device.

Beyond embedded accessibility features in software and hardware, there are many other ICTs specifically designed to assist the visually impaired. These include Braille readers, overlay keyboards, scanners and speech input/output to name a few. Indeed, such ICTs have revolutionized the way the visually impaired communicate and participate. This book looks at how these and other information and communication technologies have levelled the playing field for the visually impaired, paritcularly as it relates to including them (inclusiveness) in the democratic space, and in providing them with an equitable (equity) opportunity to participate in this space – inclusiveness and equity. Inclusiveness and equity are two important concepts in democratic speak and is today recognized as two of the critical components of good governance. The two terms generally describe 'a society for all' regardless of race, class, gender, ethnicity, or disability. In this society for all, everyone has access to the social, economic, and political processes, systems, intitutions, events and so on. As this book will demonstrate, ICTs are tools which enable this access.

This book, with its focus on inclusiveness and equity, represents one of many moments of a decade of work on how and in what ways ICT can strengthen and have strengthened democracy and promote good goverance – Participation (Waller 2013); Rule of Law (Waller and Taylor 2013); Efficient, Responsive and Effective Government (Waller and Genius 2014) as well as Transparency and Accountability (Waller 2016). My interest in the visually impaired was motivated by personal experience – my own challenge with keratoconus as well as my mother's brief experience with cataract and now glaucoma. My interest has also been motivated by my interaction with several individuals with visual impairments who, despite their dis/ability, are engaged politically and participate in the democratic process much more so than many sighted persons that I know. Through my observation, I have always marvelled at how ICTs, in particular, have contributed to the ability of these people to participate in the democratic process – equality, equity, vote, make decisions, protest, demonstrate, talk/communicate, be informed, and so on. In other words, being visually impaired has not discouraged them from 'envisioning democracy' – acting, organizing and being able to access, engage and participate in the democratic space (that area in social, economic, and political life that entails several moments, which function together synchronously, harmoniously and dialectically to preserve, strengthen, and progress democracy in a society).

This book is about the experiences of these visually impaired people. Consequently, I have intentionally used a qualitative methodology which facilitates the investigation of a phenomenon as consciously experienced by individuals, how they construct meaning, describe their objective realities, and their causal explanations of a phenomenon. This methodology is 'descriptive phenomenology' and it is further discussed in chapter 1. As a methodologist, I have ensured that the application, mechanics, and outcomes of this methodology are also demonstrated through this book for future researchers.

This book is the outcome of a research grant, which was provided to me by the Office of the Principal, University of the West Indies (UWI), Mona campus. I therefore thank the institution for this grant. I also use this opportunity to thank Senator Floyd Morris, a Jamaican politician and the Director of the Centre for Disability Studies at UWI. Senator Morris was the first blind person to become President of the Jamaican Senate. This is indeed a great accomplishment, and he is certainly a motivating force, not only for visually impaired Jamaicans, but other Jamaicans with other disabilities, as well as many other indiviudals with no disabilities. I had the pleasure of speaking with Senator Morris on several occasions during the research activities which led to this book (data collection). He is a true inspiration and a great advocate for the use of ICTs to 'envision democracy'.

Another great advocate for the use of ICTs as enablers for the visually impaired is Senator Kerryann F. Ifill who has also served as President of the Senate in Barbados. I had the distinct pleasure of speaking with Senator Ifill during the data collection stage of this project. She is a wellspring of information on the current and potential use of ICTs for 'envisioning democracy'. There are several other persons who assisted me with the data collection for this book. These include Jermaine Young, Anneke Clarke, and Mickael Graham (Jamaica) as well as Jamaro Marville (Barbados), and I thank them for their efforts.

Without sounding technologically deterministic, the experiences of these two distinguised individuals and others who were interviewed for this study is a testament to the enabling power of ICTs. Consequently, it is hoped that the readers of this book, PWDs, researchers, social workers, politicians, policymakers, academics, and so on will be motivated to explore other aspects of ICTs for PWDs to 'envision democracy'. In other words, this book is a charge for such persons to design, advance, update, take seriously, or encourage policies which enable PWDs to 'envision democracy' through the use of ICTs or promoting the use of ICTs in their daily lives or the lives of PWDs in their care to 'envision democracy'.

In preparing this book, I had to draw from different disciplines and schools of thought. It is indeed good that so many persons are researching PWDs and ICTs. Certainly, the creation of a space that allows researchers the opportunity to develop a body of work which explores this particular phenomena of the use of ICTs by persons with disability to access the democratic environment can provide researchers with an opportunity to engage and interact as well as share ideas and identify solutions to address this usually vulnerable group. It is hoped that this book will encourage further research in this area and encourage a body of knowledge that would lead to substantive policies, projects and programmes to assist, enable, and engender the inclusion and equitable participation of not only visually impaired citizens but also persons with other types of disabilities as well.

Acronyms and Abbreviations

ADA	Americans with Disabilities Act
APC	Association for Progressive Communications
APG	Association of Disabled People
BCODP	British Council of Disabled People
CDA	Combined Disabilities Association
CITO	Central Information Technology Office
CORAD	Commission of Restrictions Against Disabled People
CRPD	Convention on the Rights of Persons with Disabilities
CVSS	Council for Voluntary Social Services
DAN	Disabled People's Direct Action Network
DIG	Disablement Income Group
EGDI	E-Government Development Index
EU	European Union
GLAD	Greater London Association of Disabled People
ICT	Information and Communication Technologies
ITU	International Telecommunication Union
IYDP	International Year of Disabled Persons
JACLD	Jamaica Association for Children with Learning Disabilities
JACMR	Jamaica Association for Children with Mental Retardation
JAWS	Job Access with Speech
JCPD	Jamaica Council for Persons with Disabilities
LGBT	Lesbian, Gay, Bisexual and Transgender
MDGs	Millennium Developmen Goals
NFB	National Federation of the Blind
NVDA	Non-Visual Desktop Access
PC	Personal Computer
PVO	Private Voluntary Organizations
PWD	People with Disabilities
UN	United Nations
US	United States

UWI	The University of the West Indies
VOCODER	Voice Coder
VODER	Voice Operating Demonstrator

Chapter 1
Introduction

Background and Objectives

Considerable work has been done regarding how and in what ways Information and Communication Technologies (ICTs) have contributed to the lives of people with disability (Bonnah 2010; Aziz et al. 2011). However, not much is known about how and in what ways ICTs have contributed to the level of political participation or inclusion among the population of visually impaired in any part of the world. More so, not much is known about the role of ICTs in enabling or empowering visually impaired citizens to access the democratic space, particularly in the Caribbean. Critical issues, such as equitable participation and marginalization, and other challenges faced while attempting to access the democratic space have remained unexplored. From interacting or communicating with political representatives, to participating in voting rituals, and/or their level of activism to advocacy, the democratic needs of the visually impaired have never been addressed adequately in the disability, political or the democracy-related literature.

The inability of these visually impaired citizens to achieve such a goal is not only a violation of their human rights, but it is an indication that the democratic system is somewhat dysfunctional. Given the well-established connection between democracy, good governance, economic development, and the potential of advanced technologies to promote the inclusion of visually impaired groups to participate in the democratic space, there is an urgent need to examine the challenges of inclusion and equity faced by visually impaired Caribbean citizens and the possibilities of ICTs in addressing these challenges. This book is based on a study which explored the experiences of visually impaired persons with the use of ICTs to access the democratic space in Jamaica and Barbados. The goal of this book, therefore, is to highlight and draw attention to the experiences of Persons with Disabilities (PWDs) in Jamaica and Barbados with the use of ICTs to engage and participate in the democratic space. Within this goal were several objectives. These objectives were:

1. To understand how and in what ways ICTs have aided visually impaired Caribbean citizens to access and participate in the democratic space.

2. To determine to what extent ICTs have addressed the challenges of equity and inclusion faced by visually impaired Caribbean citizens.

3. To identify primary challenges that visually impaired Caribbean citizens experience and how ICTs aid access to and participation in the democratic space.

4. To highlight and draw attention to solutions offered by visually impaired citizens themselves to mitigate the challenges they face using ICTs to access and participate in the democratic space.

These research objectives were explored through the following research questions:

1. What has been the experience of visually impaired citizens regarding the use of ICTs to facilitate their access and participate in the democratic space?

2. To what extent have ICTs addressed the challenges of equity and inclusion faced by visually impaired Caribbean citizens?

3. What are the primary challenges that visually impaired Caribbean citizens experience with regard to the use of ICTs to access and to participate in the democratic space?

4. Based on their experiences, what solutions do visually impaired Caribbean citizens offer to the challenges they face using ICTs to access and participate in the democratic space?

Research Design

To answer the research questions, this study utilized a *qualitative descriptive research design*. This type of research design is based on the qualitative research strategy and is generally used to qualitatively explore, understand, and comprehensively describe an issue. In the case of this study, a phenomenon was being qualitatively explored – that is, the use of ICTs by visually impaired Caribbean citizens to access, engage and participate in the democratic space. Such desriptive designs are normally used in instances where little is known about the issue or phenomenon being explored. There are many different types of qualitative methodological frameworks associated with the qualitative descriptive research design. The one used for this study is *phenomenology*.

Methodology

'Phenomenology' is a philosophical discipline and methodology that is associated with the works of Edmund Husserl, René Descartes, Martin Heidegger, Jean-Paul Sartre, Maurice Merleau-Ponty, and others. Phenomenology is an approach to doing research which evolved through protest of the positivist paradigm (LeVasseur 2003; Lopez and Willis 2004). As a methodology, it is used to understand people's everyday experiences. This is done through an exploration of 'structures of consciousness', rich descriptions of lived experiences, and meanings based on the first-person point of view of participants. That is, the way experience is directed through its meaning or context toward certain objects, subjects, processes, phenomena, or systems or 'something'. These experiences include both passive (vision, perception, imagination, desire and hearing) and active (walking, participating, interacting, engaging and other actions) experiences, among other things, in the world. The central structure of an experience according to phenomenologists is its intentionality – the intentional relationship between persons and situations, environments, objects, subjects, processes, phenomena, or systems or 'something'. In so doing, phenomenology uncovers the structures of meaning behind the experiences of individuals and the essence of an experience. Expressed differently, it means being deliberate, purposive, or the 'directedness of experience', which is aimed toward objects, subjects, processes, phenomena, or systems or 'something' in the world.

Of importance to the phenomenological researcher is the context or meaning of these situations, environments, objects, subjects, processes, phenomena or systems or 'something'. That is, understanding imagination, empathy, intersubjectivity, meaning, communication, collectivity, life-world, culture, awareness, thought, reflections, desire, action, perception, emotion, and so on. Known as an inductive qualitative research, methodology phenomenology seeks to study conscious, active, and passive experiences from the first-person point of view and to unpack or reveal what is located within these experiences as they relate to a particular phenomenon. According to Linda Finlay, phenomenological researchers:

> ...generally agree that our central concern is to return to embodied, experiential meanings aiming for a fresh, complex, rich description of a phenomenon as it is concretely lived (2009, 6).

Max Van Manen (1990), quoted in G.A. Shosha (2012), states, 'phenomenological research does not develop theory; it provides insight into reality and makes us closer to the living world (32). Shosha outlines the types of questions that are normally asked by phenomenological researchers:

1.   What is this experience like?
2.   What is this or that kind of experience like?
3.   What is the essence of this phenomenon as experienced by these people?
4.   What is the meaning of the phenomenon to those who experience it?

Phenomenological research characteristically starts with concrete descriptions of lived situations, often first-person accounts set down in everyday language and avoiding abstract intellectual generalizations. The researcher proceeds by reflectively analysing these descriptions. Perhaps, ideographically first and then by offering a synthesized account, for example, identifying general themes about the essence of the phenomenon. Importantly, the phenomenological researcher aims to go beyond surface expressions or explicit meanings to read between the lines so as to access implicit dimensions and intuitions. It is this process of 'reading between the lines' which has generated uncertainty; and questioning to what extent this approach involves going beyond what the person has said and enter the realm of interpretation (Finlay 2009, 10).

Phenomenology sees its origin rooted in the works of Edmund Husserl and Martin Heidegger, described as descriptive phenomenology and interpretive phenomenology respectively. 'Descriptive phenomenology' (transcendental constitutive) is a methodology where everyday conscious experiences are described. It preoccupies itself with 'intentionality' which is the experience of thought, perception, memory, emotions, and imagination while bracketing preconceived notions of the world. Descriptive phenomenology is used when the researcher wants to describe the phenomenon under study and bracket their biases (Reiners 2012, 3). In other words, the researcher declares his or her own personal biases, politics, assumptions, and presuppositions and attempts to put them aside. Bracketing helps to 'keep what is already known about the description of the phenomenon separate from the participants' description' (Shosha 2012, 32). 'Bracketing' is therefore a way to ensure trustworthiness of data collection and analysis, also an attempt to maintain some form of objectivity of the phenomenon (Shosha 2012).

With descriptive phenomenology, researchers concern themselves with the contents of the experiences of participants. They also attempt to capture or describe the meaning given to experiences; the goal is the presupposition of phenomenological reduction. 'Reduction' is the removal of theoretical prejudices with the aim of connecting with the essence of the real phenomenon, situation and individual. Expressed in a different way, it is an examination of the phenomenon and how it was intended without causal and/or historical moment of the experience. Descriptive phenomenology is associated with philosophers such as Edmund Husserl, Herbert Spiegelberg, Sir William Hamilton, and Charles Peirce. According to Finlay, researchers utilizing the descriptive phenomenological approach say, 'They stay close to what is given to them in all its richness and complexity, and restrict themselves to making any form of assertion, which are supported by appropriate intuitive validations' (2009, 11–12).

Interpretive phenomenology specifically associated with the works of Heidegger, Hans-Georg Gadamer, and Paul Ricoeur moves beyond description 'and seeks meanings that are embedded in everyday occurrence' (Reiners 2012, 2). According to Gina Reiners (2012), interpretive phenomenology is used when the research question asks for the meaning of the phenomenon and the researcher does not bracket his/her biases and prior engagement with the question under study.

This study utilizes the descriptive phenomenology methodology. It is a methodology which has gained incredible purchase in the social sciences for its strife for rich descriptions of lifeworld or lived experiences while the researcher brackets and transcends his/her own epistemological assumptions about the world surrounding the phenomenon. The study explores the experiences of visually impaired Caribbean citizens in Jamaica and Barbados who use ICTs to access the democratic space. This study is concentrated on narratives or stories, which emerged from the data collected from the persons engaged, about their experiences with ICTs to access the democratic space.

Sample, Data Collection, and Procedures

The study sought to explore common patterns elicited from the specific experiences of 14 visually impaired citizens in Jamaica and nine in Barbados who were interviewed between June 2015 and October 2015. The interview methodology was pivotal for this study and was in keeping with the requirements of phenomenology. According to Danuta Wojnar and Kristen Swanson (2007):

An important tenet of the Husserlian approach to science was the belief that the meaning of lived experiences may be unraveled only through one-to-one transactions between the researcher and the objects of research.

These transactions must involve attentive listening, interaction, and observation to create representation of reality more sophisticated than previous understandings (173).

The interviews were conducted using a semi-structured format. Several forms of interviews were conducted. These included face-to-face interviews and telephone interviews. Each interview lasted between 45 minutes to two hours in some instances. In several instances, persons were interviewed three times to clarify emerging themes.

Data Analysis and Interpretation

The data analysis and interpretation required what Husserl calls transcendental subjectivity, which is an attempt by the researcher to disconnect from his/her own lived reality and describe the phenomenon through a process of 'bracketing'. Bracketing involves recognizing but choosing not to be influenced by personal biases or experiential knowledge. Bracketing was utilized so that the interviewer was not influenced by the description of the phenomenon. In other words, it involves inspecting and dissecting the phenomenon at a distance. In short, recognizing the interviewer's pre-conceived notions while engaging the participants and listening to their stories. Indeed, this was not difficult for the interviewers who had very little intimate knowledge of the phenomenon. In fact, many of the initial chapters had to be re-written during and after the data collection and analysis process. It was during the data collection and analysis process that a more substantive understanding of the essence of the phenomenon emerged.

Bracketing notwithstanding, some aspects of Heidegger interpretivist phenomenology did influence the study. The influence was observed especially regarding culture and social context. To some extent, and in some instances, these were taken into consideration when analysing the data. Other more substantive aspects of interpretivist phenomenology, such as attempting to discover the meaning of being was not of interest and thus, this study cannot be likened to that of an interpretivist phenomenological study. It is more descriptive in nature and outlook in terms of 'describing universal essences', a belief that the consciousness is what humans share, 'an assumption that self-reflection and "conscious stripping" of previous knowledge, help to present an investigator-free description of the phenomenon', 'the assumption that adherence to established scientific rigour ensures description of universal essences or eidetic structures' and 'the assumption that bracketing ensures that interpretation is free of bias'

(Wojnar and Swanson 2007, 175). As it relates to the 'conscious stripping' of previous knowledge, given the unit of analysis and observation, as well as the issues that emerged, there was no need to reflect on the interviewer's own experiences as it would not have influenced the understanding and analysis. The process was, strictly speaking, one of discovery. Furthermore, most researchers using any phenomenological methodology, whether descriptive or interpretivist, are certain that overlapping between both approaches is expected (Shosha 2012; see also Fochtman 2008).

The particular data analysis and interpretive process was based on the strategy developed by Paul Colaizzi (1978), which is still used today (see Shosha 2012; Sanders 2003; Speziale and Carpenter 2007). This strategy is outlined in figure 1.1 below:

Figure 1.1: A Summary of Colaizz's Strategy for Phenomological Data

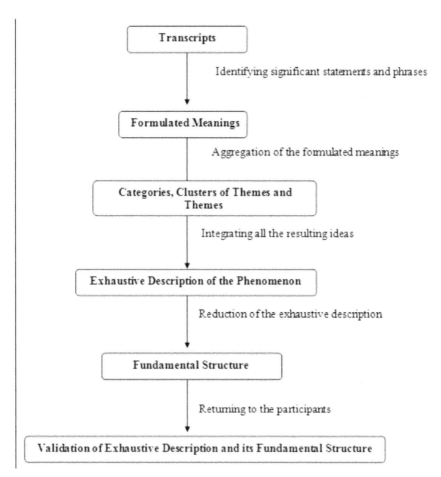

Colaizzi (1978)

From this process, the themes associated with the experiences of these citizens with the use of ICTs to access the democratic space were uncovered. The process allowed a better understanding and description of the directed awareness (intentionality) of the perceptions and experiences of the visually impaired citizens being explored, as well as the essence of their engagement with this technology. These are presented in chapters 5 and 6.

Unit of Analysis

This study focuses on the use of ICTs as tools to access the democratic space – that area in social, economic, and political life that entails several moments which function together synchronously, harmoniously and dialectically to preserve, strengthen, and progress democracy in a society. These moments include: institutions of government (the executive, the legislature, and the judiciary); standards; and principles or rules of democracy which need to be recognized. The overarching principles of democracy embrace the separation of powers, checks and balances, good governance (inclusion, equity, accountability, transparency, responsiveness, recognizing the rule of law and human rights, participation and so on) and processes or practices which are ways of acting or organizing a society in accordance with the principles of democracy, and most importantly, actors who are the citizens of a country (Keane 2009). Key to the efficient functioning of the democratic space is the principle of democratic governance and the practice of democratic processes.

Democratic processes are activities, actions, or discourses (ways of acting and organizing). These include participating in activities to strengthen democracy such as voting, decision-making exercises for example, participatory budgeting, citizen journalism, rallies, and so on. It can also include not taking bribes, being accountable for one's actions, recognizing the human rights of individuals, and observing the rule of law. It can also mean working in an efficient and effective way as a government employee and interacting with citizens in a manner that promotes a pleasant experience, for example, good service delivery. Such processes help to facilitate economic and social development of and progress within a society.

Democratic governance is the principles, standards, and rules that shape a society's way of being. It is who you are as a person and what your beliefs are. According to Carolyn Pedwell and Diane Perrons, democratic governance:

seeks to promote greater participation of marginalised groups within political processes, through addressing inequalities associated with gender, class, race, ethnicity, caste, disability and sexuality, among other variables, and greater accountability of governments towards those who have traditionally been excluded from political action (2007, 8).

Robert A. Dahl (1998) identified five standards that exist in the democratic space. These include:

Effective participation: Before any policy is developed by an association, all the members must have equal and effective opportunities for making their views known as to what the policy should be.

Voting equality: When the moment arrives at which the decision about policy will finally be made, every member must have an equal and effective opportunity to vote, and all votes must be counted as equal.

Enlightened understanding: Within reasonable limits as to time, each member must have equal and effective opportunities for learning about the relevant alternative politics and their likely consequences.

Control of the agenda: The members must have the exclusive opportunity to decide how and, if they choose, what matters are to be placed on the agenda. Thus, the democratic process required by the three proceeding criteria is never closed. The politics of the association are always open to change by the members, if they so choose to.

Inclusion of adults. All, or at any rate, most adult permanent residents should have the full right of citizens that are implied by the first four criteria (38).

Dahl summarized the advantages of democratic governance as:
1. Preventing rule by cruel and vicious autocrats;
2. guaranteeing citizens fundamental rights;
3. ensuring a range of personal freedoms;
4. providing maximum opportunity for self-determination;
5. promoting peace;
6. promoting prosperity;
7. political equality;
8. human and economic development, and
9. moral autonomy.

The principles of 'equity' and 'inclusiveness' are central to democratic governance and critical for strengthening the democratic space. Equity is a term usually used to describe justice, fairness or social inclusion. For the purpose of this book, however, equity is defined as the creation of conditions that ensure that all people have the opportunity to receive quality education services; thereby significantly reducing the effects of inequalities based on socio-economic status, disability and ethnic, cultural and gender discrimination (Organization of American States 1995, 1).

Inclusiveness is defined as the characteristics of a system such that political exclusion is avoided (Reynal-Querol 2005). In other words, it means to include people or things in a whole. According to the United Nations (UN), for equity and inclusiveness to be achieved, all members of society should be treated equally and have support from the society as a whole for improving their well-being. All segments of a society must be included in its democratic processes, treated equitably, and be free to participate and influence political outcomes without suffering any form of bias or various forms of retaliation.

Unfortunately, this is not the case in many parts of the world, particularly among many developing and new/emerging democracies. In these societies, many people do not have a voice in the democratic space. Many groups are still either excluded from, or, not treated fairly in the democratic space. Furthermore, they either do not or cannot participate, deliberate, or collaborate on issues that shape and affect their own lives. In instances where they actually do participate, they are restricted in several ways. These groups include women, racial minorities, the poor, diverse people, and especially the disabled. The disabled are particularly excluded from the democratic space. And many enabled citizens do not readily recognize or seek to include them as this does not form part of their principle.

Many people with disabilities are unable to:

1. Participate in political activities and rituals such as elections; working in, and contributing to electoral campaigns and organizations;
2. Attend demonstrations, protests, and marches; take part in the conduct of public affairs;
3. Access (engage, communicate, deliberate) their political representatives, run for public office, or hold an office at various levels of government;
4. Be guaranteed fundamental rights (not seen as equal under the law) – rule of law;
5. Serve on local elected or appointed boards; or
6. Participate in the governance system at the community level.

This suggests that visually impaired citizens in many countries around the world are either excluded from the democratic space or are unfairly treated. In other words, this vulnerable group is not provided a space to participate in the decision-making that affects them. This speaks to the challenges of equity and inclusiveness.

There is a growing body of research which has highlighted that citizens are provided with many avenues/opportunities, processes, and tools to maintain such standards – to be treated equitably, to be included in the decision-making process, to vote, to participate, and to be enlightened. These tools, processes, and avenues enable citizens to participate in their own governance, contribute to the decision-making process of government, to be heard and to interact with their representatives (Caldow 2004). Essentially, through these tools they are able to meet these standards. This book will focus on one of these tools – information and communication technologies (ICTs).

The Role and Potential of ICTs for Democracy

Historically, technologies that facilitate information and enhance communication have helped to transform the democratic space. Examples include the printing press, the postal service, the telegram, the telephone, the radio, and the television. These tools have been beneficial, particularly, to vulnerable groups such as the disabled. The benefits are focused on providing them with an opportunity to engage representatives as well as receive information about issues related to democratic governance. For example, the radio has been very instrumental in transmitting political information to visually impaired individuals. So too has television, as it relates to hearing-impaired individuals (with the help of sign language professionals). ICTs are no different.

Information and communication technologies are defined as a range of tools and technologies that use technology to gather, communicate, store, retrieve, exchange, process, analyse, and share information. Through these ICTs, an opportunity exists today, more so than a decade ago, to enhance citizen engagement, involvement, and participation (D. F. Norris 2010). ICTs have 'created immense opportunities for new forms of government-citizen communication' (Freeman and Quirke 2013, 142). Such technologies enable marginalized groups like the disabled to participate in the democratic process and encourage among the disabled and the enabled alike, the understanding of the principles of democratic governance. The next section will explore briefly the potential of this tool for promoting democracy.

ICTs enable the disabled to access and interact with politicians and critical government agents, access government information necessary to help them in their day-to-day lives, contribute to the decision-making process, participate in political activities, monitor and report on violations in the democratic system, campaign and run for public office, among other things. Examples of this include websites used to access important information or the use of email services or social media to engage political actors. Thus, ICTs can enable as well as accelerate the inclusion of persons with disabilities in economic, social, and political life (International Telecommunications Union 2012; 2013).

With ICTs, 'citizens are enfranchised through advanced technologies and communicative abundance' (Freeman and Quirke 2013, 142). They are more involved, engaged, and they participate in democratic government and the political process (Mossberger, Tolbert, and McNeal 2008). The use of ICTs to enhance democracy 'is a significant development which has been globally accepted as a democratic revolution in terms of citizen's participation in democratic activities' (Nchise 2012). This process is referred to as electronic democracy or e-democracy for short. Abinwi Nchise is correct in saying the 'perceived value and prospects of e-democracy has received extensive coverage in research and practice with the reportage of several case studies on e-democracy implementation all over the world' (2012, 165). Unfortunately, however, no substantive scholarly research project has been undertaken to explore the use of ICTs to either include the disabled in the democratic space or facilitate their ability to participate equitably in this space. This study addresses this gap in the literature.

Outline for This Book

This chapter provides the introduction to this book, which consists of the goals and objectives of the study, the research design, and introduces the conceptual framework which is further explored in chapter 2. Chapter 2 presents the conceptual framework for the book – the network of linked concepts, which flow from an objective, that are used to construct what we have come to understand as 'electronic democracy' or 'e-democracy'. These concepts include types of political institutions, political principles, political processes/practices/actions and political tools used in the information superhighway to facilitate democracy: e-parliament, e-justice, e-participation, e-voting, e-campaigning and so on.

Chapters 3 and 4 explore the existing challenges typically faced by the disabled generally and visually impaired citizens in particular, as they try to navigate the democratic space by contextualizing the challenges, mitigation strategies and outcomes associated with enabling and empowering visually impaired individuals as it relates to legislations, projects, programmes, and tools/technologies. Chapter 3, in particular, presents as well as evaluates the mitigation strategies that have emerged since the year 2000, particularly in relation to engendering participation and the inclusion of people with disabilities in the political space. In addition, the chapter highlights the international approach that has been spearheaded by international organizations, as well as country level approach that has been influenced by the United Nations. Chapter 4 provides a look at the types of technologies that have and can enable and engender inclusion and equity of persons with disability. Both chapters help to establish a historical context that builds on the conceptual framework presented in chapter 2 and, which was used to guide this study.

Chapters 5 and 6 discuss the findings of the study. More specifically, chapter 5 presents the findings from several interviews that were conducted with visually impaired individuals in Jamaica and Barbados. The chapter also draws on literature, which captures the experiences of persons who are visually impaired in North America, Europe, New Zealand, as well as parts of Africa, Asia and Latin America. More specifically, the chapter focuses on several issues surrounding how and in what ways ICTs have contributed to the lives of visually impaired citizens in these countries, particularly as it relates to accessing the democratic space. Chapter 6 explores the primary challenges that visually impaired Caribbean citizens face with regard to the use of ICTs to access and participate in the democratic space. In this chapter, some solutions to these challenges are also explored.

The concluding chapter, chapter 7, summarizes the findings of the study and explores emerging innovations in ICTs that are appropriate to visually impaired individuals in terms of empowering them to engage and participate in the democratic space.

Conclusion

It is hoped that this book will help to sensitize stakeholders in the democratic process to the challenges of inclusion and equity faced by visually impaired Caribbean citizens, through the experiences of persons interviewed for this study. It is also hoped that this book will help to provide guidelines from the success stories and lessons learnt in Jamaica and Barbados regarding the inclusion and equitable participation of the visually impaired Caribbean nationals in the democratic process through the use of appropriate and inexpensive technology related mitigation strategies. Finally, I hope that this book will also help to (1) increase the pool of citizens participating in the democratic process; (2) initiate a discussion among stakeholders regarding disability mainstreaming not only as it relates to democratic participation but other spheres of social life; (3) increase the awareness of policymakers regarding technologies that can increase the participation of disabled people; and (4) provide a template and a model for addressing the challenges of inequity and lack of inclusion of visually impaired citizens globally.

Chapter 2
E-Democracy:
Fostering Inclusion and Equity

Introduction

In the first chapter, the challenges that people with disability face as well as the mitigation strategies at the global and country levels were explored. While there have been some substantive gains in the social and economic space, particularly where empowerment and inclusion are concerned, there are still some critical problems relating to the ability of people with disabilities entering the democratic space to engage the democratic process. This chapter explores some possible solutions that have emerged over the last decade to deal with this problem. Attention is also drawn to ICTs as a tool that can enable the disabled to operate within the democratic space. As mentioned in the previous chapter, this process is called e-democracy.

This chapter discusses the rituals associated with e-democracy in order to illustrate how this practice can contribute to the political life of people with disabilities, particularly visually and hearing-impaired citizens.

Fostering Inclusion and Equity with e-Democracy: Ways of Strengthening Democracy

On May 4, 2011, the UK *Guardian* newspaper published an article entitled, 'Helping more disabled people get into politics: A new scheme aims to encourage more disabled people into politics and develop a cross-party network of ambassadors.' The article portrayed a worrisome situation where persons with disability appear to be excluded from the democratic space as part of the electorate and more so, as a member of the possible elected. Such a predicament is the norm in many countries around the world with regard to people with various forms of disabilities. As previously mentioned, the democratic space is vast. It is a structure that entails several moments, which function synchronously, harmoniously, and dialectically to preserve, strengthen, and advance democracy in a society. These moments include institutions of government; principles, norms, or rules of democracy which need to be recognized; processes or practices of the citizens of a country. The democratic space also includes 'tools' that aid practices and principles and provide people with access to instructions and other actors to achieve or enable democracy. In the next section, we will look at how one of these tools – ICTs – enables, connects, and holds together the many moments of the democratic space.

Political Institutions

Political institutions are a very important moment of the democratic space. They are physical and non-physical established and embedded systems of rules that structure interactions. Therefore, political institutions are seen as a broad spectrum of things that include, but are not limited to: political parties, agents, organizations, and agencies of government and the state, charters, conventions, political groups, and even language. They are thus entities that create, structure, organize, monitor, maintain, enforce and mediate government policy, rules, procedures, and principles of a society. In a democratic society or in a democratic space, these actions and their outcomes are aimed at promoting, maintaining, and strengthening democracy. Institutions are structures that matter the most in a society. They make up the fabric of social and political life. In politics, institutions are salient, well established, and acknowledged by most members of a society. Political institutions create expectations about how citizens should act and organize themselves. These political institutions both enable and constrain behaviour, and they also shape and are shaped by political behaviour or political practices.

Examples of political institutions include political parties, trade unions, and organizations of the state such as legislative, executive, as well as judicial offices. They also include artefacts and well-established conventions. Children are instructed by political institutions through the agents of socialization such as the family, education system, media, and groups. It is through these agents of socialization that children recognize and accept political institutions and learn to interact with these institutions. In the democratic space, all citizens are allowed access to these institutions on a daily basis for democracy to function effectively. That, however, is not the case for people with disabilities. Given the interrelated nature of these components of democracy and these elements of the democratic space, very often, when some citizens do not have access to this space there is a fissure which can damage the configurations of the democratic space. This exclusion usually occurs in many ways. Some examples include: (1) being excluded from joining political parties, trade unions, or other organizations of the state; (2) not being able to engage political leaders, documents of democracy, or justice (not accessing the executive); and (3) not having the avenues to be acquainted with the rules and laws of the land – not accessing parliaments, not accessing the judiciary.

Political institutions shape economic growth and development, but can also be affected by these variables. Secure and strong political institutions contribute to stable markets and thus, growth and development. Such governments can protect the contracts and protect property rights. Discussions regarding the type of political institutions are still being debated (Peet and Hartwick 2015; Robinson 2006).

Political Principles

Political principles are fundamental truths. They are propositions that are the basis of a behaviour, system, or belief. In the political space, they are essentially the norms, values, and beliefs about the political configuration of a political system. However, in the democratic space, they are the norms, values, and beliefs about the political configuration of democracy and mechanisms as well as the operations of a democratic society. The more substantive principles of the democratic space are those of democratic governance or good governance. Good governance is defined as the participatory, efficient, and effective management of a country's human, natural, economic, financial, and other resources and affairs that are transparent, responsive, inclusive, accountable, and based on the principles of value consensus. Some of the most prominent principles within the democratic space are the principles of good governance, respect for the rule of law and human rights, free and fair elections, equality, and justice for all and fairness. Figure 2.1 outlines the principles of good governance.

These principles are globally accepted, institutionalized, and well-recognized in many democratic societies. Governments of most democratic societies as well as civil society, private sector institutions, and international organizations operating in democratic countries also promote these principles. Yet, despite the efforts of these organizations to preserve, strengthen, promote and encourage democratic principles, there are many persons who reside in democratic societies who do not share nor believe in these principles. This is particularly the case with many disabled people living in these societies. They do not share these principles because they have grown to believe that their disability makes them incapable of actively participating in the democratic space. Many persons with disability believe that they are unable to access political institutions and that political principles do not apply to them. The belief is also promoted by the fact that many abled citizens sometimes, either intentionally or unintentionally, make persons with disability feel invisible. They sometimes have initiatives or activities that do not facilitate or cater for people with certain disabilities. One example of this is the absence of Braille policy documents on even critical problems which even affect the visually impaired, in several countries around the world.

Figure 2.1: Principles of Good Governance

Participation

Participation by both men and women is a key cornerstone of good governance. Participation could be either direct or through legitimate intermediate institutions or representatives. It is important to point out that representative democracy does not necessarily mean that the concerns of the most vulnerable in society would be taken into consideration in decision-making. Participation needs to be informed and organized. This means freedom of association and expression on the one hand and an organized civil society on the other hand.

Rule of law

Good governance requires fair legal frameworks that are enforced impartially. It also requires full protection of human rights, particularly those of minorities. Impartial enforcement of laws requires an independent judiciary and an impartial and incorruptible police force.

Transparency

Transparency means that decisions taken and their enforcement are done in a manner that follows rules and regulations. It also means that information is freely available and directly accessible to those who will be affected by such decisions and their enforcement. It also means that enough information is provided and that it is provided in easily understandable forms and media.

Responsiveness

Good governance requires that institutions and processes try to serve all stakeholders within a reasonable timeframe.

Consensus oriented

There are several actors and as many view points in a given society. Good governance requires mediation of the different interests in society to reach a broad consensus in society on what is in the best interest of the whole community and how this can be achieved. It also requires a broad and long-term perspective on what is needed for sustainable human development and how to achieve the goals of such development. This can only result from an understanding of the historical, cultural, and social contexts of a given society or community.

Equity and inclusiveness

A society's well being depends on ensuring that all its members feel that they have a stake in it and do not feel excluded from the mainstream of society. This requires that all groups, but particularly the most vulnerable, have opportunities to improve or maintain their well-being.

Effectiveness and efficiency

Good governance means that processes and institutions produce results that meet the needs of society while making the best use of resources at their disposal. The concept of efficiency in the context of good governance also covers the sustainable use of natural resources and the protection of the environment.

Accountability
Accountability is a key requirement of good governance. Not only governmental institutions but also the private sector and civil society organizations must be accountable to the public and to their institutional stakeholders. Who is accountable to whom varies depending on whether decisions or actions taken are internal or external to an organization or institution. In general, an organization or an institution is accountable to those who will be affected by its decisions or actions. Accountability cannot be enforced without transparency and the rule of law.

Source: United Nations Economic and Social Commission

Political Processes, Practices, or Action

Political processes, practices, or political action within the democratic space is appreciated as both a principle of the democratic space as well as a political practice. Political practices are those actions by citizens or political actors that are used as enablers of the political space. These democratic practices therefore operate as the nexus between the people and the political institutions. There are many ways in which people enact political processes. These include voting, protesting, volunteering, attending political rallies, attending political events, writing letters or petitions, and other forms of engagement. Inaction can also be a process. Inaction occurs when an individual decides not to participate for whatever reason. One of the most common forms of inaction is political apathy.

Inaction can also occur when persons are unable to access the relevant institutions or disbelieve a particular truth. One example of this, in a democracy, is the disbelief that one is able to participate in the democratic system. This is sometimes the case with people with disabilities. Many people with disabilities are unable to participate in various political processes. For example, the hearing impaired are sometimes unable to gain the benefits of attending political rallies, particularly those who do not have a sign language expert. Those with physical challenges are sometimes unable to participate in many political processes such as campaigning, and in some countries around the world are even unable to vote.

Political Tools

In a democracy, tools, artefacts, or paraphernalia are physical items that are used to enhance an element of the democratic space. Political tools can be many things and perhaps anything and are often not defined as such, but can be articulated or represented as 'political tools'. For example, the paper is a basic tool, which can be used for doing many things; writing, typing, printing, painting, or drawing is a popular activity. The paper becomes a political tool when the writing, typing, printing, or drawing is of a political nature – to, among many things, encourage, demonstrate, or promote action, thought or philosophy. Another example of the politicization of a tool within the context of this book is the use of the cane by a disabled individual to navigate into the House of Parliament to participate in some way, or to go to a polling station to vote. Other examples of tools being used for political purposes include the use of a hearing aid by someone with a hearing impairment to listen to political speeches or debates or through the use of the television or other media to share information about the other components which make up the democratic space.

In a democracy, tools such as the television, radio, and newspapers have traditionally played a tremendous and important role by facilitating democratic and political socialization. These tools allow communication between and among various democratic spaces and principles, processes, and people. Tools such as ICTs bring the democratic space together and are used to send and retrieve information about democracy. They are used to access, facilitate, encourage and/or engage political actors and political intuitions. Most recently, information and communication technologies (ICTs) have been identified as tools which can significantly allow the disabled to access the democratic space in terms of addressing the challenges often faced by people with disabilities and thus allowing them to access the democratic space. No doubt, such a discourse suggests that ICTs can indeed strengthen democracy. The next section explores how and in what ways ICTs can be used in this regard.

It is important to recognize the dialectic and intertwined nature of these components of the democratic space. Although each component serves a specific purpose they are intertwined and dependent on each other for the effective functioning of democracy. They operate as a network to strengthen democracy. The next section will focus more closely on ICTs as part of this network and how ICT enhances the other components of the democratic space to strengthen democracy.

Information and Communication Technologies as a Political Tool

As noted earlier, ICTs are defined as a range of tools that use technology to gather, communicate, store, retrieve, exchange, process, analyse, and share information. ICTs generally include: computers and wireless devices, peripherals and storage instruments; software applications; network infrastructures, and the technical protocols they require such as SMTP, TCP/

IP, FTP; particularly significant are security (SSL) and privacy (P2K) protocols for e-commerce and commercial surveillance (cookies etc.) as well as legal and regulatory frameworks such as patents and copyright (i.e., these are not contextual to ICT: they are integral). Since early 2001, there has been a plethora of research and interest in the use of these technologies to navigate the democratic space and to strengthen democracy by promoting political actions and processes, and in so doing, offer all citizens access to the democratic space and institutions. This synergy is referred to as electronic democracy or e-democracy. Chapter 1 outlined some elements of this synergy to introduce the conceptual framework. In the next section this framework – e-democracy – is discussed along with some other elements of e-democracy to complete this framework.

e-Democracy

The study locates itself within the epistemological and ontological conceptual space of electronic democracy (e-democracy). E-democracy is a term currently en vogue since the popularity of the ICT for development discourse some 20 years ago. For the purpose of this book, however, 'electronic democracy' (e-democracy), is defined as 'the use of ICTs with the aim of providing increased opportunities for citizen participation and involvement in the decision-making process in order to meet growing citizens' expectations' (Hacker and van Dijk 2000, 200). In other words, and more simply put, it is the use of ICTs in enacting democratic processes to encourage the principles of democratic governance.

E-democracy is thus a complex term used to connote the use of ICTs to broaden and deepen democracy by enabling citizens to engage, participate and contribute to, support, as well as to be involved in the democratic process. E-democracy, therefore, is a means of strengthening the mechanisms of democratic governance. As a sort of bottom-up approach to strengthening democracy, e-democracy allows citizens, civil society, governments, and businesses to gather and share information, participate in opinion formation as well as decision-making. E-Democracy thus facilitates an informed and engaged citizenry, which represents the core principle of democracy (Beddie, Macintosh, and Malina 2001). Such a process encourages political openness and consequently leads to promoting transparency and accountability through monitoring and evaluation with the use of ICTs (Wong and Welch 2004; Coleman and Blumler 2009; C. G. Riley 2003; Macintosh and Whyte 2006). Thus, the real aim of e-democracy is to provide citizens with a wide choice of options and avenues for them to participate in the democratic process and also to provide them with the notion that their participation can make a difference.

The term e-democracy is usually confused with e-government and e-governance and sometimes wrongly used interchangeably. This was a point raised by D.F. Norris (2010) who argues that whilst the terms are intertwined they are different and not synonymous as suggested by much of the literature. Whereas electronic government is the use of ICTs for the purpose of making government more efficient and effective as well as improving public service delivery; e-governance is much broader than e-government. E-governance incorporates e-government but also includes other aspects of enhancing the democratic process. Examples include e-administration (the use of ICTs to automate their internal operations and business processes) and e-society (the use of ICTs by citizens, business, civil society, and communities to engage issues of governance) as well as e-government (the use of ICTs to make government more efficient and effective, to enhance service delivery, and to disseminate as well as gather information to and from business, government, and society). With e-governance citizens have some regulation, power, and control over the affairs of government business and society.

E-democracy is an even much broader term encompassing e-governance and thus e-government, e-society, e-administration as well as other discourses such as e-parliament, e-justice, e-participation, e-voting, e-security, e-campaigning, e-procurement and e-petition.

e-Parliament

The World e-Parliament Report 2008 defines e-Parliament as 'a legislature that is empowered to be more transparent, accessible, and accountable through ICT, and which empowers people, in all their diversity, to be more engaged in public life by providing greater access to its parliamentary documents and activities'. E-Parliament is a means of empowering people to be more engaged in public life by providing them with access to parliamentary actors, agents, documents, and activities. It is a means of facilitating an equitable and inclusive information approach to support the primary functions of parliament specifically as it relates to shaping the policies, laws, and programmes of a nation. ICTs also provide citizens with a way to monitor and evaluate parliamentary processes, outputs, and outcomes. In other words, e-Parliament allows people to have a say in how they are governed. Many e-Parliament initiatives help raise citizen awareness of the decisions of parliament, and these initiatives also facilitate a space for citizens to be actively engaged in parliamentary debates as well as content formulation.

E-Parliament allows persons with disabilities the ability to access information in many ways. The visually impaired can use their mobile phones, tablets, laptops, or personal computers (PCs) to access legislations, comment on legislations, or to monitor and evaluate parliamentary processes, outputs, and outcomes using special Braille technologies for input. These technologies include a Braille keyboard, Braille display, and a Braille printer. A Braille keyboard is an input device that allows users to type text or instructions for the computer in Braille. Braille displays are technologies that are connected to a computer. The display reads the screen text and presents it to users through the Braille display. A Braille printer embosses raised braille dots onto Braille paper. Output technologies include software which read the computer screen to the user. These are called text-to-speech software. Examples of such software are Readplease, Readclip, and Read4me. Many operating systems developed by Microsoft and Apple as well as word processing applications also provide these output services for users. Hearing-impaired citizens can also use their mobile phone, computer, or tablets to read parliament proceedings or watch parliamentary debates with the closed caption feature of their output device turned on.

e-Justice

Electronic justice can be described as the use of ICTs in the field of justice to improve citizens' access to justice and effective judicial action. Through e-justice, citizens can assess information on the function of the legal system, they can locate and interact with lawyers as well as judges to seek advice on legal matters, governance, rules, and the legal system. E-justice also facilitates collaboration between and among lawyers, civil society, individuals, legal actors, and courts. E-justice allows for electronically connecting courts to facilitate the exchange of information about cases and to conduct trials with participants from different locations. Barry Walsh (2011) lists 14 advantages of e-justice. According to Walsh (2011, 2–12), e-justice will:

1.   ... give us electronic filing, which will help speed up the disposition of cases.
2.   ... overcome the problem of errors being made in the court registry in recording the details of cases.

3. ... overcome the problems [of] court registries, where staff sometimes deliberately go slow in registering cases and ask for bribes recording the details of cases.

4. ... overcome problems in processing the assessment of court fees to be paid and the methods for collecting those fees.

5. ... overcome the problem of accurately recording what is said in court, by giving us an audio recording and a transcript.

6. ... give us the option of video conferencing, so that witnesses and prisoners need not physically attend a court to give evidence.

7. ... enable us to record all court decisions and make them available for all to see on the Internet.

8. ... provide our court with a tool that judges may use to research law and improve the quality of their decisions.

9. ... utilize email and other messaging services, which will overcome our problems in delivering paper claims on defendants and in notifying parties of court hearings.

10. ... help us reduce our staffing costs, as computer systems need fewer operators than paper systems.

11. ... give us digitized court files (scanned records), which will allow us to get rid of paper files.

12. ... give us a paperless office, so that judges and staff work entirely using computer screens to save on printing costs.

13. ... put all our services on the Internet, so that we will not have to provide services to those who will not use a computer.

14. ... help the court to take control of its large caseloads, using databases and up-to-date case information to make better decisions about case management.

It is undeniable that courts around the world, especially those in the developing world can significantly benefit from the implementation of e-justice programmes and projects. Indeed, e-justice offers visually and hearing-impaired citizens several options to access information regarding the legal system. Emails can be used to locate and interact with lawyers as well as judges. The aforementioned input and output devices can be used to engage legal actors to get advice on legal matters, governance, rules, and the legal system. The technologies can allow persons with physical disabilities to access the courts via video and teleconferencing technologies such as Skype and other such online services.

e-Participation

E-participation has become an important lexicon of the social sciences today (Funilkul and Chutimaskul 2009; Sæbø, Rose, and Flak 2008). Though there are many different interpretations and definitions of e-participation, the one offered by Abinwi Nchise (2012) is emblematic of the popular use of the term by scholars researching and writing about e-participation and captures the relationship between e-participation and e-democracy. According to Nchise (2012):

> E-participation can principally be understood as technology-mediated interaction between the civil society and the formal politics and administration sphere of government making processes support for citizen involvement in deliberation and decision... The main purpose of e-participation is to enhance citizen's involvement in political deliberation and decision-making process with the aid of technology. Social and political practices such as voting, political deliberation, petition writing, political campaigning and other forms of political discourse mediated by information and communication technology (ICTs) falls under the field of e-participation and hence are referred to as e-democracy applications (169).

E-participation is on the rise in countries all over the world. In Europe, for example, there are several structured projects and programmes in various institutions within and across Europe that are dedicated to facilitating and empowering citizens to participate in public decision-making, policymaking and the political processes of their governments as well as the European Government (European Commission 2009). These projects have ranged from facilitating online mediation for representatives and citizens to promoting online voting on critical issues within countries across Europe as well as providing a space for online decision-making on politics. They have also covered issues such as consumer protection law, climate change, cyberbullying, child abuse, identification (ID) theft, file sharing, open thread and the financial crisis (Chrissafis and Rohen 2010). Thanassis Chrissafis and Mechtild Rohen believe that this has had 'far reaching transformation of institutional and political functions' (2010, 89).

E-participation offers persons with disabilities an array of options to participate in the democratic process. For example, it allows the visually impaired the opportunity to participate in online discussions regarding the state of their nations. It makes the hearing impaired believe in the principle of inclusion by helping them keep their politicians accountable through emails and blogs or that they can monitor the affairs and transactions of government agencies through websites that provide information on expenditures and contracts. E-participation provides people with disabilities the opportunity to act or engage in political practices such as protests through online protests and demonstrations. Persons can access political institutions through web-portals, provide feedback on bills, or possibly ask questions. In some instances, disabled citizens, like other citizens, are able to interact with political leaders through special chat capabilities and they can work together through emails, as well as instant messaging on political documentation that can add to the decision-making process of government. Indeed, e-participation has the potential to facilitate the involvement and engagement of persons with disabilities in the democratic space.

e-Voting

Electronic voting is the use of ICTs to provide citizens with the opportunity to cast ballots. This can either be done via electronic mail, over an Internet server, or electronically at a particular site. It is what P. Norris (2004) calls a method of bringing citizens closer to the polls. The literature identifies three general ways of bringing the people closer to the polls (Stratford and Stratford 2001; Abramson and Morin 2003; Done 2003; A-M. Oostveen and Van den Besselaar 2004; Alvarez and Hall 2003; Carter and Bélanger 2012). These are 'poll site Internet voting', 'kiosk voting', and 'remote Internet voting'. Poll site Internet voting involves the casting of ballot at specially identified polling sites managed by polling officers. The voters have the option of choosing where to cast their votes from a number of sites. Kiosk voting offers voters the opportunity to cast their votes at I-voting machines located at convenient locations such as schools, malls, libraries, and so on. These sites are also managed by polling officers. Remote Internet voting allows voters to cast ballots virtually at any location that has Internet access whether it is in their home, workplace, or an Internet café located anywhere in the world. These I-voting strategies have been identified as a convenient, cost-effective, and efficient method of strengthening democracy in the twenty-first century (Gibson 2001; 2005; Carter and Bélanger 2012).

E-voting, improves accessibility and provides persons with disability the opportunity to participate in what is considered the most substantive form of democracy – voting. Through e-voting, specifically Internet voting, visually, hearing or physically disabled persons can conveniently cast their ballots from the comforts of their home rather than attempting to traverse a sometimes obstacle riddled journey to the polling station. For those who do decide to make the journey, there are new e-voting technologies, which make voting for the hearing and visually impaired voters convenient. These include e-voting machines, which read out options for visually impaired voters or direct recording electronic (DRE) touch-screen voting terminals. E-voting is already a reality in several parts of the world and has provided persons with disability with the means to participate in the democratic process through action and inculcate specific principles making them believe that they are a part of the democratic space. In this regard, e-voting therefore helps to strengthen the democratic process.

e-Security

Many nations today are dependent on advanced information and communications technologies to manage their operations. Though this has contributed to the efficient and effective management of government resources, and has trickled down to improve service for citizens, it can also put a nation at risk. Criminals now have the power to disrupt critical national infrastructure and industries by hacking into government information system and modify, steal, or delete information. E-security provides solutions designed to ensure that the confidentiality, integrity, and availability of electronic information are protected against malicious attackers (World Bank 2011, 1). E-security can range from providing security for browsers, networks, files, operating systems, or any form of data encryption through a combination of techniques such as cryptographic methods and protocols. E-security is an important aspect of the e-democracy/e-governance configuration because it helps to build trust and confidence in government's e-government initiatives. Privacy and security are usually two very important concerns for citizens in the information age. According to S.E. Colesca (2009):

> Concerns about inadequate security and privacy safeguards in electronic networks can lead to distrust in applications of e-Government that might pose risks, such as through unwarranted access to sensitive personal information or vulnerability to online fraud or identity theft (7).

More recently, R. Palanisamy and B. Mukerji observe that over the years, citizens have become concerned about 'cyberspace identity thefts and privacy violations' (2012, 237). They further postulate that 'citizens may be sceptical and mistrust e-government services, perceiving them as invasions of citizens' security and privacy'. Throughout the years, similar observations have been made by G. James (2000), Z. Ebrahim et al. (2003), Karen Layne and Jungwoo Lee (2001), and Jeffrey Seifert and G. Matthew Bonham (2003). Citizens today are bombarded by the media with images and sounds of easy access to personal records electronically, frequent accounts of credit card fraud and identity theft. This has created a culture of fear among many net-citizens and potential net-citizens. The risk or fear of cybercrime is often a deterrent for citizens' participation in e-government activities. Citizens need to be confident that their transactions are secure, private, and that their information is protected. Very little information exists regarding issues surrounding e-security and people with disabilities specifically and provides an opportunity for further research.

e-Campaigning

Electronic campaigning involves the use of ICTs to publicize a cause, solicit support, or influence the decision-making process of a group, individuals, or an organization by disseminating information quickly. It is often used to contact, engage, inform, as well as mobilize large groups of individuals. E-campaigning has become a major tool used by politicians, international organizations, governments, and NGOs. Political parties are now implementing e-campaigning as a tactic that forms a part of their overall political strategy (Williams and Serge 2014). Examples of this include the 2005 general election campaign in the UK (Stanyer 2005), the 2009 European Parliament elections (Vergeer, Hermans, and Sams 2013), and the 2008 US presidential race (Williams and Serge 2014). For political parties, e-campaigning is generally regarded as a critical tool. It is inexpensive, allowing parties access to a large number of persons in a relatively short period of time.

E-campaigning is increasingly becoming a tool of choice for several other groups and organizations. For example, civil society groups and activities have also used e-campaigning tools as a means of strengthening democracy. The reachability and inexpensiveness of this tool make it an ideal mechanism to publicize a cause. Examples include the Drop Haiti's Debt (2010), Green My Apple (2006), Make Poverty History (2005), Oxfam GB (2001–2004), Amnesty International UK (2008) awareness campaigns (Raymond 2010). E-campaigning certainly can and has been an activity undertaken by people with disabilities. Indeed, hearing and physically impaired citizens (as well as assisted visually impaired citizens) can participate in this ritual by simply retweeting a tweet by a political party, group, or individual on Twitter or reposting a campaign advertisement (text, video, or image) on Facebook or other social media platforms. They can also themselves construct ads and/or engage/solicit votes or participation from other net-citizens.

e-Petition

Electronic petition or e-petition is the use of ICTs by citizens to raise awareness, marshal, and/or express popular support around a political issue and engage public officials regarding the particular issue through digital signatures (Panagiotopoulos and Al-Debei 2010; Mosca and Santucci 2009). It is a form of public participation that helps the citizenry express themselves, and in some instances, influence the decision-making process, and overall, directly contribute to and participate in the democratic process. Indeed, e-petitions, like their offline counterparts, have the potential to create change, foster participation, and strengthen democracy.

According to Peter Cruickshank et al.:

> In the area of political participation, petitioning is a simple yet effective tool which provides a first step for citizens who want to interact with and influence democratically-elected assemblies (2010, 2).

E-petitions can be submitted either via a web-based interface or via electronic mail. Daria Santucci (2007) notes that ICTs are encouraging the practice of petitions more than ever before, and so, e-petitions are seen as a transformative force in modern democracies by promoting participatory democracy (Lindner and Riehm 2008). MoveOn.org, Avaaz iPetitions, Petitions Online and Change.org are examples of some of the world's largest petition platforms. E-petitions are slowly becoming the new form of activism in the industrialized world and in many developing countries as well. E-petitions sometimes originate from within government but it is often a construct of civil society (Lindner and Riehm 2009).

Many of the aforementioned activities facilitate a combination of information, consultation, participation, civic engagement, and dialogue between and among citizens, government, civil society, and even businesses. All of these activities are important to strengthening democracy. Citing the Organisation for Economic Co-operation and Development (OECD) (2003), Julie Freeman and Sharna Quirke (2013) explain this:

> Information' is a one-way relationship where governments produce and distribute information to citizens, such as occurs through websites and e-newsletters. This includes active attempts by governments to increase information dissemination on particular issues and arbitrary citizen access to information available through digital means upon demand. 'Consultation' involves a limited two-way process through which citizens can provide feedback to governments; for instance, via online surveys and petitions. This requires that citizens are provided with the information necessary to make informed decisions, but feedback is restricted to

topics predetermined by governments, which means civic input has a limited capacity to shape political agendas and discourse. 'Participation' concerns the development of stronger relationships between citizens and governments, in which citizens are viewed as partners. It includes active involvement of citizens in the policy-making process and may take place through the use of, for example, digital discussions and wikis, where citizens can propose policy options and shape the direction of political dialogue (143).

Unlike traditional bricks and mortar petitioning, which can sometimes mean a citizen physically travelling from one place to the next and is considered a trans-temporal activity, e-petitioning can be spatio-temporal. The citizen does not have to move and locate himself or herself at a particular place. The convenience of the e-petition makes it attractive to many people. Beyond the convenience, the extensive reach of the e-petition makes it a powerful democratic tool. There is supporting evidence from countries such as Britain and the United States demonstrating the benefits of e-petitions. For people with disabilities, e-petitions eliminate many of the challenges associated with physical movement thereby allowing them to participate in e-petition exercises.

e-Procurement

Electronic procurement is the business-to-business, business-to-consumer, business-to-government, consumer-to-government purchase and sale of goods and services by or through electronic means. E-procurement involves several other activities through electronic means such as tendering (e-tendering), vendor purchase order and catalogue management, invoicing (e-invoicing), contract management (e-contracts), and e-payments. Within the context of e-democracy, e-procurement citizens are able to go online and access government services such as paying taxes, paying for records, or downloading information. This translates to the elimination of long lines as well as enhancing transparency and accountability. The latter of which is accomplished by removing the one-on-one human exchange between the citizen and government worker.

Beyond the actual transactions associated with e-procurement, many websites allow citizens to monitor the financial activities of governments. Examples of this include contract awards and the employment of persons. This is perhaps one of the greatest advantage of e-procurement and one of its contributions to democracy. This empowers citizens with the ability to track and monitor government financial processes using their laptops, phones, and other ICTs. For many persons with a disability, e-procurement provides an opportunity to undertake government related transactions. Additionally, it also empowers participation in the monitoring and evaluation of government related activities.

Strengthening Democracy through E-Democracy: Some Examples

According to Freeman and Quirke (2013), 'e-democracy can be understood as ongoing digital civic participation activities that partially disperse governmental power in order to enable the public to actively influence political decision-making' (143). The importance and popularity of the concept 'e-democracy' and the rituals associated with it, as well as the social practices among scholars and practitioners are inherently linked to the many ways in which e-democracy can strengthen various aspects of democratic governance. Indeed, in the last decade we have seen several examples of e-democracy in practice. Some of these include:

1. The development of special websites and software to make it easy for people with disability to participate in the democratic process, to access information about government systems, processes, institutions, events, actors and information pivotal to themselves, engage parliamentarians and other agents of the state.

2. The use of websites to enable people from rural communities to interact with and keep in touch with decision-makers in their metropolis.

3. The use of online consultation and deliberations between and among decision makers and their citizens.

4. The use of online petitions (e-petitions) by citizens regarding issues of concern to them.

5. The use of the Internet in Scotland by political parties as well as individual candidates during parliamentary elections to disseminate information to potential voters as well as to engage them in discussion about politics (Baxter and Marcella 2013).

6. The use of social media among activities, citizens, and social movements to voice their opinions (Waller 2013).

7. The use of ICTs by governments to promote greater active civic participation and involvement among citizens specifically youth through the use of crowdsourcing.

8. The use of Internet technologies by activists to enrich and facilitate collective action and increase the range of activist/social movement repertoire.

9. The use of crowdsourcing in Iceland to gather citizen input for the purpose of shaping constitutional reform.

10. The use of blogs, personal, organization and party websites to provide citizens with politically critical and timely information.

11. The use of social networking sites such as Facebook by politicians to enrich the two-way dialogue between themselves and citizens in Germany (Wandhoefer, Thamm, and Joshi 2011).

12. The use of Twitter to increase engagement and share information with 'traditionally "hard to reach" groups such as disabled, lesbian, gay, bisexual, transgender and hidden communities' (Freeman and Quirke 2013, 146).

13. The use of social media by politicians to reach out to potential voters with the view of encouraging them to go to the polls (Kelly 2007).

14. The use of social media by governments to reach out and connect with citizens and gain insights about policies and programmes (Hull, West, and Cecez-Kecmanovic 2010).

15. The use of virtual hall town meetings by politicians to connect thousands of people to a single virtual forum with the aim of deliberating issues and get feedback on policies from citizens (Taylor-Smith and Lindner 2009).

16. Citizen-led online activism.

17. The use of mobile phones as monitoring tools to ensure free and fair elections.

18. The use of social media such as Facebook and Twitter to talk (Waller 2010).

Conclusion

As illustrated above e-democracy now represents a critical means of strengthening democracy (OECD 2001; Kingston 2007; Hilgers and Ihl 2010; Macnamara 2012). It is slowly becoming a permanent feature (in thought and practice) of most democracies or those aspiring for democracy. E-democracy allows citizens to become more included and involved in the democratic and political process and elected representatives with an opportunity to interact with their constituency. E-democracy provides citizens with the means to fair and impartial access to information that is necessary to better understand, integrate with, and engage the democratic process. It also provides the possibility for citizens to exercise some form of control over the decision-making process or government and/or government agencies.

E-democracy should not be seen as a technological panacea nor a form of technological determinism. Rather, it is a network of actors, discourses, systems, institutions, structures, and processes all working together towards strengthening democracy, democratic governance, and practice. It is an additional channel or a tool for widening the choices available to citizens, governments, the private sector, and civil society (specifically political parties, non-governmental organizations, and international partners) for democratic participation, involvement, deliberation, consensus building, engagement, and practice. E-democracy can therefore help to increase inclusiveness of and accessibility to the democratic process, achieve transparency and accountability of government as well as the efficiency, responsiveness, and effectiveness of government. In addition, e-democracy can help to restore the declining interest in politics and the democratic process as well.

Citizenry is central to the e-democracy framework. Therefore, e-democracy allows citizens the opportunity to transcend from being mere customers to owners. They are able to participate in the decision-making process through blogs, wikis, and emails. They can access information in real time regarding critical aspects of political life and can become politically engaged citizens (*citoyen*). E-democracy facilitates democratic involvement through unmediated discussions over the Internet using phones and laptops, direct representation and participation, as well as enabling civic contributions that impact on decision-making (Coleman and Blumler 2009).

Chapter 3
Enabling the Disabled:
Challenges, Mitigation Strategies and Outcomes

Introduction

Despite the many policies in several countries around the world, persons with disability still feel excluded from the social, economic, and particularly the political space. This chapter explores the challenges generally faced by the disabled as they try to navigate these spaces. The chapter will also present the limited literature regarding mitigation strategies that have emerged since the year 2000; particularly, vis-a-vis engendering participation and the inclusion of people with disabilities in the political space. The international approach that has been spearheaded by the United Nations (UN) as well as the country level approach that has been influenced by the UN is also discussed. Although these countries do not represent the breath of country level policies and programmes that empower, include, and enable the disabled, they do represent the sort of activities that are happening across many regions of the globe. This chapter therefore represents the contextual framework for the study.

The Disabled

Like most concepts the term 'disability' is a complex and controversial word that is constantly evolving and perpetually contested. The term 'disability' or 'the disabled' or 'people with disability', used interchangeably in this work, all have the same meaning. Over the years, definitions have evolved from the physical and intellectual to even the social. The definition also changes depending on where you are located. For example, if you are living in the United States, the Americans with Disabilities Act (ADA) defines a person with a disability as:

> a person who has a physical or mental impairment that substantially limits one or more major life activity. This includes people who have a record of such an impairment, even if they do not currently have a disability. It also includes individuals who do not have a disability but are regarded as having a disability (ADA 2013).

In New Zealand, disability is defined as:

> any self-perceived limitation in activity resulting from a long-term condition or health problem; lasting longer or expected to last longer than six months or more and not completely eliminated by an assistive device (Statistics New Zealand 2006).

In Jamaica, a disability is 'any restriction or lack of ability to perform an activity in the manner or the range considered normal for a human being. Such restriction or lack of ability must be as a result of impairment' (PIOJ 2009). Persons who have lost a significant portion of their vision can be located within this definition.

The World Health Organization (WHO) which defines disability as:

> an umbrella term, covering impairments, activity limitations, and participation restrictions. An impairment is a problem in body function or structure; an activity limitation is a difficulty encountered by an individual in executing a task or action; while a participation restriction is a problem experienced by an individual in involvement in life situations.

> Disability is thus not just a health problem. It is a complex phenomenon, reflecting the interaction between features of a person's body and features of the society in which he or she lives. Overcoming the difficulties faced by people with disabilities requires interventions to remove environmental and social barriers (WHO 2012).

This definition is accepted in many countries around the world and, intertextually as well as interdiscursively, represents many other definitions used by the aforementioned countries. It is the definition observed for this study.

Disability covers many different impairments. These include physical disabilities, namely, those that limit the physical function of an individual, such as limitations in limbs that impair motor ability. It also includes sensory disability such as impairment of vision and hearing as well as olfactory and gustatory impairment (impairment of the sense of taste and smell). Disability also covers intellectual disability (a range of mental/cognitive deficits), non-visible or invisible disabilities (such as sleep disorders, narcolepsy, epilepsy, fibromyalgia, asthma, and even diabetes).

Developmental disability as well as pervasive developmental disability both fall into the general definition of disability. Developmental disability refers to problems with growth and development such as spina bifida and other congenital medical conditions. Pervasive developmental disabilities are based on socialization and communication issues and include childhood disintegrative disorder, autism, and Asperger syndrome. Somatosensory impairment (insensitivity to stimuli such as heat, touch, pain, and cold) is also considered a disability. This work focuses on the sensory disabilities of vision and hearing impairment. However, this chapter focuses on disabilities generally but with a bias towards these sensory disabilities.

The Plight of the Disabled

More than one billion people in the world live with some form of disability (WHO 2011, xi). According to the UN (2011), the 'most pressing issue faced globally by persons with disabilities is not their specific disability, but rather their lack of equitable access to resources' (UN 2011, vii). These resources include education and health, legal and social services, social life, economic opportunities, and the democratic space. According to the WHO (2011):

> The onset of disability may lead to the worsening of social and economic well-being and poverty through a multitude of channels, including the adverse impact on education, employment, earnings, and increased expenditures related to disability.
>
> Children with disabilities are less likely to attend school, thus experiencing limited opportunities for human capital formation and facing reduced employment opportunities and decreased productivity in adulthood.
>
> People with disabilities are more likely to be unemployed and generally earn less even when employed. Both employment and income outcomes appear to worsen with the severity of the disability. It is harder for people with disabilities to benefit from development and escape from poverty due to discrimination in employment, limited access to transport, and lack of access to resources to promote self-employment and livelihood activities.
>
> People with disabilities may have extra costs resulting from disability – such as costs associated with medical care or assistive devices, or the need for personal support and assistance – and thus often require more resources to achieve the same outcomes as non-disabled people. This is what Amartya Sen has called "conversion handicap". Because of higher costs, people with disabilities and their households are likely to be poorer than non-disabled people with similar incomes.
>
> Households with a disabled member are more likely to experience material hardship – including food insecurity, poor housing, lack of access to safe water and sanitation, and inadequate access to health care (10).

The WHO (2011) further stated that '[p]overty may increase the risk of disability.' It has been well established in the literature that persons with disabilities have 'disproportionately high rates of poverty' (UN 2011, vii; see also Gwatkin et al. 2007). According to this UN publication:

Certainly, if one goes into the poorest urban slum or the most marginalized rural village and asks 'who is the poorest person in your community'? one will almost invariably be directed to the household of a person with a disability (2011, vii).

This has been established in the literature for some time now (See Moyes 1981; Brittan 1982; Doyal 1983; Reith 1994; Groce et al. 2011). In Jamaica for example, up to July 2014, '10 per cent of Jamaicans are disabled and 82 per cent of persons with disabilities were living below the poverty line' (*Jamaica Observer* 2014). According to Statistics New Zealand, in 2013, 24 per cent of the New Zealand population were identified as disabled. This is a total of 1.1 million people (Statistics New Zealand 2013).

Poverty is often regarded as a cause and consequence of people with disabilities. Additionally, poverty and disability reinforce each other. The consequences are exclusion, inequity, and vulnerability for people with disabilities. For example, in many instances, someone who is visually impaired from birth would have challenges accessing the education system. This often renders them unable to find employment/gainful employment and consequently this lack of employment threatens the livelihood of the disabled individual leading to poverty. The disability helps to exacerbate poverty in many ways. It increases economic strain for the disabled individual and also affects their family as well. Poverty renders the disabled incapable of mitigating his or her ability to be adversely affected. In instances where the disabled is the primary caregiver the general household and their specific dependents are affected due to the possibility of poor nutrition, limited access to healthcare, maternity or mental care, dangerous living conditions (bad sanitation and poor hygiene), or lack of access to education (all circumstances that can lead to disabilities). Breaking out of this vicious cycle is almost impossible.

Poverty can lead to a disability and being disabled has led to poverty both within a generation and across generations. Even before embarking on a review of the literature revealing this dialectic relationship, the first focus group for this study, though not represented in the data, exposed the phenomenon. This focus group was used as a pilot to organize the study. The motivation of the study was to gather information about whether, how, and in what ways the disabled engaged the democratic space, and the role of ICTs in facilitating such an engagement. The focus group was arranged by the coordinator of a local association with a disability programme in Montego Bay, Jamaica. The coordinator was asked to gather 11 participants for a focus group session sometime in October 2014. Nine visually impaired individuals between the ages of 30 and 65 attended and participated. As the interview progressed, it was clear that the only engagement that some of them had with the democratic space was on election day when a family member or a political party representative took them to the voting station. It was also clear that ICTs played no role in their lives other than to communicate with friends and families over a mobile phone, which included an occasional discussion about different aspects of politics.

Two things were abundantly clear from that focus group. The first being that too few people appreciate the luxuries of the lives they lead in being able to access and enjoy basic amenities. The second is that this may not have been the best demographic to engage about the use of ICTs in accessing the democratic space. What was also clear from the engagement was the cruel connection between poverty and disability. One participant divulged that she had difficulty providing for her child. Her inability to see had prevented her from accessing effective healthcare for her child who had suffered a birth defect and this eventually led to him becoming hearing impaired. And no doubt this may in the future contribute to his inability to access education and secure a job to maintain his livelihood as well as others around him.

The women in the focus group presented their situation as more dire than the males. This is true of disabled women and girls globally as women with disabilities suffer more than males (Hanna and Rogovsky 1991; Nosek et al. 2001). There are many representations of this phenomenon across the globe. For example, according to a publication by the group Women with Disabilities in Australia, 'Women with disabilities face particular disadvantages in the areas of education, work and employment, family and reproductive rights, health, violence, and abuse. They are usually victims of sexual, domestic violence, neglect, discrimination, and physical abuse' (WWDA 2012).

The report further stated:

> Two million women with disabilities live in Australia, making up 20.1% of the population of Australian women. Women with disabilities continue to be one of the most excluded, neglected and isolated groups in Australian society, experiencing widespread and serious violations of their human rights. As a group, they experience many of the recognised markers of social exclusion – socioeconomic disadvantage, social isolation, multiple forms of discrimination, poor access to services, poor housing, inadequate health care, and denial of opportunities to contribute to and participate actively in society (p. 12)

The report listed the number of challenges experienced by women with disabilities in Australia. Based on the literature reviewed, the challenges disabled women in Australia encounter can be said to represent the challenges faced by women with disabilities globally. These are outlined below in figure 3.1 with particular emphasis on the struggles and triumphs of women with disability.

Figure 3.1: The Challenges that Women with Disability Face

- women with disabilities experience violence, particularly family violence and violence in institutions, more often than disabled men;

- gender-based violence, including domestic/family violence, sexual assault/rape is a cause of disability in women;

- women and girls with disabilities are often at greater risk than disabled men, both within and outside the home, of violence, injury or abuse, neglect or negligent treatment, maltreatment or exploitation;

- women with disabilities are more vulnerable as victims of crimes from both strangers and people who are known to them, yet crimes against disabled women are often never reported to law enforcement agencies;

- more women than men are classified as disabled, particularly as ageing populations mean that larger proportions of the elderly are women with disabilities. Of all household types in Australia, elderly single women are at the greatest risk of persistent poverty, with more than half of elderly single women living in poverty;

- women with disabilities are less likely to receive service support than disabled men;

- while disabled people are much more likely to live in poverty, women with disabilities are likely to be poorer than men with disabilities;

- women with disabilities and men with disabilities have different economic opportunities, with disabled women less likely to be in the paid workforce than disabled men. They also have lower incomes from employment than men with disabilities. In Australia, the gender gap in pay has widened over the last four years. Superannuation savings are directly linked to paid work, and current average superannuation payouts for women are less than half that received by men;

- gender biases in labour markets have meant that disabled women's productive potential is less effectively tapped than disabled men's and that disabled women have been more concentrated than disabled men in informal, subsistence and vulnerable employment;

- over the last decade, the unemployment rate for disabled women in Australia has remained virtually unchanged (8.3 per cent) despite significant decreases in the unemployment rates for disabled men;

- employment of women with disabilities in the Australian public sector shows an employment rate of approximately 2.8 per cent, compared to that of men with disabilities of 3.9 per cent;

- women with disabilities are more likely to be sole parents, to be living on their own, or in their parental family than disabled men;

- women with disabilities, with less financial resources at their disposal than disabled men, are particularly vulnerable to living in insecure or inadequate housing;

- women with disabilities and their children are more likely than disabled men, to be affected by the lack of affordable housing, due to the major gap in overall economic security across the life-cycle, and to their experience of gender-based violence which leads to housing vulnerability, including homelessness;
- women who become disabled after marriage are at higher risk of divorce than disabled men and often experience difficulty maintaining custody of their children;
- women with disabilities who are parents, or who seek to become parents, face barriers in accessing adequate health care and other services for both themselves and their child[ren];
- women with disabilities are more likely than disabled men, to face medical interventions to control their fertility;
- women with disabilities experience more extreme social categorization than disabled men, being more likely to be seen either as hypersexual and uncontrollable, or de-sexualized and inert;
- media images contribute to the presumptions that the bodies of women with disabilities are unattractive, asexual and outside the societal ascribed norms of 'beauty';
- women with disabilities have significantly lower levels of participation in voter registration and election, in party politics and thus, in governance and decision making at all levels compared to men with disabilities;
- women with disabilities like other women, share the burden of responsibility for unpaid work in the private and social spheres, including for example, cooking, cleaning, caring for children and relatives. Women in Australia spend almost three times as many hours per week looking after children as men; and do two thirds of the unpaid caring and domestic work in Australian households;
- women with disability from ethnic or indigenous communities are more likely to have to contend with forces that exclude them on the basis of gender as well as disability, culture and heritage; and
- women with disabilities are more exposed to practices which qualify as torture or inhuman or degrading treatment (such as sterilization, forced abortion, violence, forced medication, chemical restraint).

Source: Women with Disabilities in Australia 2012, 8–12.

A similar if not worse situation exists in India. For example, Sharma (2014) wrote, 'Treated worse than animals: abuses against women and girls with psychosocial or intellectual disabilities in institutions in India,' which documented the abuses of women and girls with intellectual and psychosocial disabilities at institutions. The report highlighted abuses of rights, verbal and physical violence, and neglect in these institutions. In several countries around the world, particularly in the developing world, there are many other recorded instances in which women and girls suffer similar challenges. The next section highlights several strategies that have been implemented over the years to address the challenges faced by people with disability.

Enabling the Disabled: Some Solutions

In 1976, the United Nations General Assembly proclaimed 1981 as the International Year of Disabled Persons (IYDP) under the theme 'full participation' and mandated a plan of action for people with disabilities at the national, regional, and international levels. This plan of action would, among many things, promote equity, inclusion and access for people with disabilities, as well as provide avenues to empower this segment of society.

The objectives of the year included raising public awareness about the challenges of the disabled and what can be done to address these challenges. The objectives were also centrally focused on encouraging persons with disabilities to come together and develop action plans to improve their lives as well as to increase the awareness of the utility of persons with disabilities across societies and to promote an understanding of people with disabilities.

One of the main outcomes of the IYDP was the development of an action plan – the World Programme of Action Concerning Disabled Persons. This action plan was adopted by the UN General Assembly in December 1982 and promoted the theme, 'Equalization of Opportunities'. The World Programme was a global strategy harnessed from a human rights perspective that was designed to promote, among other things, the equality for and the full participation of people with disabilities in the social and economic life of a country. Several activities specifically related to prevention of disability, rehabilitation, and equalization of opportunities (full participation of people with disabilities) were recommended under the action plan aimed at engendering the theme of equalizing the disabled which were to be implemented in countries around the world. According to the UN (2005), the implementation of the World Programme of Action:

> ... would entail long-term strategies integrated into national policies for socio-economic development, preventive activities that would include development and use of technology for the prevention of disabilities, and legislation eliminating discrimination regarding access to facilities, social security, education and employment. At the international level, governments were requested to cooperate with each other, the United Nations and non-governmental organizations (1).

In 1983, the UN announced the 1983–92 the United Nations Decade of Disabled Person. The UN expected countries and other organizations to implement the recommendations of the World Programme of Action during the decade. During that period and shortly after, the United Nations continued its efforts to empower and include the disabled in social life.

The activities include the Convention on the Rights of the Child (1989), and the Standard Rules on the Equalisation of Opportunities for People with Disabilities (1993).

By 2006, the United Nations Convention on the Rights of Persons with Disabilities (CRPD) was adopted and was entered into force May 2008. According to the UN, the Convention is recognized as the most extensive recognition of the human rights of persons with disabilities. The purpose of the CRDP has been to 'promote, protect, and ensure the full and equal enjoyment of all human rights and fundamental freedoms by people with disabilities and to promote respect for their inherent dignity' (WHO 2011, 9). To this end, the CRDP promoted:

1. respect for inherent dignity, individual autonomy including the freedom to make one's own choices, and independence of persons;

2. non-discrimination;

3. full and effective participation and inclusion in society;

4. respect for difference and acceptance of persons with disabilities as part of human diversity and humanity;

5. equality of opportunity;

6. accessibility;

7. equality between men and women;

8. respect for the evolving capacities of children with disabilities and respect for the right of children with disabilities to preserve their identities (ibid.).

By 2011, the UN continued its efforts to promote the inclusion of people with disability with the publication 'Disability and the Millennium Development Goals'. The publication essentially provided a guide for disability service providers (persons working in the field of disability), advocates, and others working with people with disability on how to include the disabled in the planning, monitoring, and evaluation of millennium development goals (MDG)-related programmes and policies. Though the MDGs did not explicitly focus on individuals with disabilities, more recent discussions suggest that all millennium development goals include people with disability, and many governments and organizations have accepted this.

Since the Convention and the World Programme of Action Concerning Disabled Persons, there has been an upsurge in policies and programmes at the global and local levels. These policies and programmes have been geared towards including the disabled in the political space, both as the electorate and the elects.

A more recent publication, 'Digital Dividends: Bridging the Disability Divide through Digital Technologies', recognizes the power of ICTs:

ICT is clearly identified as an enabler in the Convention on the Rights of Persons with Disabilities.... The Convention (2006) consistently brings up the role of ICT in promoting the independence and full participation of persons with disabilities across life domains, and requires States Parties to make concerted efforts and investments to advance access to ICT. ICT is an important enabler of accessibility to systems and services (Article 9), access information and uphold freedom of expression and opinion (Article 21), and meaningful habilitation and rehabilitation (Article 26). Articles on access to justice, rights to political participation, education, health, and employment all raise the need of affordable and accessible technology to realize the rights of persons with disabilities. ICT is a disruptive force in enabling the inclusion of persons with disabilities due to a number of characteristics (Deepti Sament Raja 2016).

Raja provides a snapshot of the main barriers that persons with various disabilities face and also provides examples of ICT solutions that can address those barriers: This is presented in table 3.1:

Table 3.1: Barriers to Participation by Disability Type and Relevant Solutions

Disability Category	Examples of barriers in social, economic, and community participation	Examples of accessible technology solutions
Visual Disability Includes total blindness or low vision	• Reading print (e.g., textbooks, instructions, documents) and writing (e.g., signing checks, legal documents) • Accessing visual information in print or audiovisual media (for example, warnings and information in text scrolls on television). • Navigating new surroundings when all signage is in text.	• Text-to-speech rendition and speech/voice output • Braille displays • Screen and text magnification • Voice recognition • Audio description of graphic and visual media • Electronic audio signage • GPS-facilitated navigation • Optical character or image recognition • Changing screen brightness, colour contrast
Hearing disability Total or partial hearing loss	• Hearing lessons, warnings, and other auditory information in person or over audio media such as the radio or television. • Communicating with others including educators, peers and colleagues, clients, first responders, government personnel, and others.	• Closed and open captioning, subtitles for videos, TV programming • SMS, text messaging • Text Telephone or Telecommunication Device for the Deaf (TTY/TDD) which allow text messaging over the phone line • Telecommunications Relay Services which allow text to speck conversions through an operator • Use of vibrations/text alerts instead of audio alerts

Disability Category	Examples of barriers in social, economic, and community participation	Examples of accessible technology solutions
Speech impairments	• Communicating with others including educators, peers and colleagues, clients, first responders, government personnel, and others.	• SMS, text messaging • Synthesized voice output, text to speech functionality • Use of virtual picture board and communication solutions
Physical Disability Loss of mobility, dexterity, and control over some body functions.	• Entering, navigating, and using buildings, classrooms, and other physical spaces. • Using writing tools such as pens and pencils, keyboards, mouse.	• Voice recognition systems • Adapted and virtual keyboards • Joysticks and adapted mouse • Use of eye-gaze and gestures to control devices • Remote and online access to work, education, and other services
Cognitive Disability Includes a range of conditions which may impact a person's memory, thinking and problem-solving, visual, math reading and language comprehension, ability to pay attention or follow instructions. Examples of underlying conditions are traumatic brain injury, learning disabilities, down syndrome, autism, cerebral palsy.	• Difficulty understanding, remembering, or following instructions. • Difficult in comprehending textual information. • May occur together with other limitations such as speech impairments or trouble with hand grip and movements. • Difficulty in communicating or expressing thoughts and ideas.	• Text-to-speech rendition and speech/voice output • Touch screen devices • Mobile apps and online resources that mimic Augmentative and Alternative Communication (AAC) devices, electronic picture boards for communication • Organization and memory aid tools such as online calendars, note taking, alerts • GPS-facilitated navigation • Use of multimedia to aid comprehension e.g., videos, graphics
Psychosocial Disability	• Need for flexible schedules • Difficulty understanding, remembering, or following instructions. • Inability to react and make appropriate decisions following information or instructions. • Difficulty in communicating or expressing thoughts and ideas.	• Use of online communication, documentation, work tools to aid with flexible scheduling • Organization and memory aid tools such as online calendars, note taking, alerts

Country Level Approaches

Many of the policies of international organizations have trickled down to the country level with many countries around the world implementing several of these policies and initiatives. This section highlights initiatives in several countries that promote the empowerment and inclusion of people with disabilities as well as those that seek to address inequalities between disabled and non-disabled people. The countries that are explored in this section were selected based on the author's familiarity with these countries.

United States of America

The United States Government has undertaken several key initiatives aimed at empowering and facilitating the inclusion of persons with disability in economic, social, and political life. These are governed by several acts which include the Rehabilitation Act, the Individuals with Disabilities Education Act (IDEA), National Library Service for the Blind and Physically Handicapped, Randolph-Sheppard Act, Javits-Wagner-O'Day Act, Voting Accessibility for the Elderly, the Handicapped Act, the Americans with Disabilities Act (ADA), as well as the Help America Vote Act. These legislative enactments have guided many initiatives in the US, which prohibit any form of discrimination on the basis of disability in the state, government services, employment, and commercial related activities as well as transportation, telecommunication, and accommodation. Many organizations across the country have adopted several elements of what these legislations try to address in their operations. The landmark 1990 Americans with Disabilities Act extended civil rights protection to people with disabilities.

Under the ADA, businesses operating within the US are mandated to facilitate the accommodation of people with disability. This has meant, for example, redesigning office spaces to meet the needs of people with disability. The ADA also forced changes in the public space: transportation systems were upgraded to make them more accessible to people with disabilities, and telecommunication services were modified to offer adaptive services. The legislation created an atmosphere that facilitated the integration, inclusion, and participation of people with disability in the public and economic social space of American society.

Today, many Americans with disabilities enjoy living independent and self-affirming lives. Several initiatives, guided by the legal and regulatory framework and championed by disability advocates have significantly contributed to this. There are, however, many Americans with disabilities who still face discrimination, prejudice, bias, and injustice. Despite the successes on the social and economic front, not many persons with disabilities participate in a substantive way in the political space and only a rare minority of these rise to public life. For example, according to Lisa Schur et al. (2013), during the 2012 US presidential elections, generally speaking, there were several 'difficulties faced by many people with disabilities in exercising the right to vote' as '[A]lmost one-third (30.1%) of voters with disabilities reported difficulty in voting at a polling place in 2012' (1–2). Undoubtedly, persons with disabilities in the US still face issues of access and inclusion.

New Zealand

The facilitation of minorities and persons with disability in New Zealand are well entrenched in the New Zealand society. The road towards an inclusive and enabling environment for people with disability in New Zealand has been guided by several policy and strategy documents. The most substantive have been the Disabled Persons Community Welfare Act 1975; the Industrial Relations Act 1973, the New Zealand Disability Strategy 2000/2001, the New Zealand Sign Language Bill 2004, and more recently, the Disability Action Plan 2014–2018. Other documents which have been instrumental in empowering the disabled as well as encouraging their inclusion in the New Zealand society include; 'Pathways to Inclusion: Improving Vocational Services for People with Disabilities' published by the New Zealand Department of Labour in 2001 and 'To Have An Ordinary Life: Kai Whai Oranga Noa: Community Membership for Adults with an Intellectual Disability' published by the New Zealand National Health Committee. In addition to these local documents, at the international level, the New Zealand Government signed the Disability Convention on March 30, 2007. Consequently, several initiatives to empower people with disability in New Zealand and facilitate their inclusion in New Zealand life are also guided by these international standards.

In the last decade, guided by these local and international standards, New Zealand has seen the emergence of several institutions that have sought to improve the lives of people with disabilities. These have included the Office for Disability Issues, which leads the implementation of New Zealand's disability policies as well as monitors the New Zealand Disability Strategy and other disability related issues. This also includes the Human Rights Commission, the Ombudsman, and the New Zealand Convention Coalition, the three of which play a pivotal role in monitoring the UN Convention on the Rights of Persons with Disabilities (Disability Convention).

One of the champions of people with disability in New Zealand is the Minister of Disability Issues. Among other things, the Minister oversees the New Zealand Disability Strategy. The Minister reports to Parliament annually on the progress of implementation of the New Zealand Disability Strategy. The New Zealand Disability Strategy has been a guiding document for addressing the challenges of the people with disabilities in New Zealand.

Two decades of advocacy work have resulted in the significant advancement of persons with disability in New Zealand. This is specifically the case as it relates to providing them access to transportation, the physical environment, information, accommodation, communications, and other social services as well as ensuring that disabled people live with dignity. Despite these advances, however, like many parts of the world, there are many New Zealanders with disability who are still disconnected from the political space. In a 2012 report of the New Zealand Human Rights Commission entitled 'Political participation for everyone: Disabled people's rights and the political process' it was recognized that 'New Zealand's existing voting and political systems are not designed for everyone' (P. Gibson and Manning 2013). The report further stated that:

Disabled New Zealanders experience barriers to exercising their rights to vote and participate politically such as inaccessible information and voting papers, limited voting methods, and a lack of accessible buildings and services enabling engagement with politicians (1).

Indeed, this undermines the ability of the disabled to successfully occupy and contribute to the democratic space in New Zealand. Work continues to address this gap in the New Zealand democratic space.

United Kingdom

At the end of the First World War, Britain witnessed an influx of two million newly disabled British ex-servicemen, particularly the visually impaired. Almost immediately, the attitudes towards the disabled changed and the government started to play a more active role in addressing the needs of people with disability. Perhaps one of the earliest pieces of legislation in this period was the Blind Persons Act. Promulgated in the 1920s, the Act provided economic support for visually impaired Britons. Since then, a series of legislations and strategic documents have emerged and have contributed to the empowerment and inclusion of people with disability in the UK. These include the 1944 Disabled Persons Employment Act, and the National Health Service Act, and National Assistance Act, both passed in 1948. By 1970, the Chronically Sick and Disabled Persons Act was passed, followed in 2005 by the Disability Discrimination Act. The UK Government ratified the United Nations Convention on the Rights of Persons with Disabilities as well as passed the Single Equality Act in 2010.

In addition to the legal and regulatory framework, the disability movement in the UK has been a very active one. Over the century, several associations, institutions, and initiatives have been established and are aimed at empowering, including, and enabling the disabled. These have included the Greater London Association of Disabled People (GLAD) established in 1951, the Disablement Income Group (DIG) founded in 1965, the Association of Disabled People (APG) established in 1971, the formation of the Union of the Physically Impaired Against Segregation in 1974, Sisters against Disablement founded in 1977, Disabled People's International, the Commission of Restrictions Against Disabled People (CORAD) and British

Council of Disabled People (BCODP) were established in the early 1980s. By the mid to late 1980s, the Preston and South Ribble Access and Mobility Group and the first Black Disabled People's Association were established. The 1990s saw the establishment of Disability Awareness, Regard (a movement established to challenge the exclusion of lesbian, gay, bi-sexual and transgender [LGBT] persons with disability), Disabled people's Direct Action Network (DAN). The last decade has seen the establishment of the Disability Rights Commission, and in 2005, the then Prime Minister of Britain established a Strategy Unit out of which the publication, 'Improving the Life Chances of Disabled People' provided guidelines and recommendations for achieving disabled people's equality by 2025.

Though much has been done to enable, empower, and include the disabled in the UK, based on a recent article by Paul Dodenhoff in *Disabled World* entitled, 'The UK General Election 2015: What's in Store for Disability?' much more still needs to be done, particularly the inclusion of the disabled in the democratic space (Dodenhoff 2015). Despite what has already been accomplished (United Response 2010) there are still many Britons with disabilities who are still politically excluded.

South Africa

Among the developing countries, South Africa has a sizable share of people with disabilities and across the world (developing and developed) persons with disability constitute a sizable proportion of the world's population.

South Africa is a signatory to the United Nations Convention on the Rights of Persons with Disabilities as well as the Optional Protocol to the Convention on the Rights of Persons with Disabilities. Disability issues are recognized by the legal and regulatory system in South Africa; for example, the South African Constitution prohibits unfair treatment and discrimination against people with disabilities. The Employment Equity Act, the Social Assistance Act, and the Skills Development Act address issues of exclusion, disparities in income, occupation and employment within the national labour market and are extended to people with disabilities. Additionally, plans to address South Africans with disabilities were expressed in a 1997 White Paper 'Integrated National Disability Strategy: White Paper'.

These policies, the legal and regulatory framework, and the initiatives have encouraged engendering an environment where people with disability can fully participate in economic and social life or be able to occupy the democratic space (Dube 2005).

The Caribbean

Jamaica

Attempts to empower, include, and facilitate the equality of the disabled in Jamaica has expanded beyond the traditional focus on healthcare, rehabilitation, or charity to that of a serious policy discourse on inclusion and access through the country's Vision 2030 National Development Plan and the passing of the Disability Act in 2014. Jamaica has a population of 2.9 million people of which approximately seven per cent are living with a disability. The Development Plan and the Act were both informed and guided by the Convention on the Protection of the Rights of Persons with Disabilities which Jamaica signed in 2007. For the most part, many of these persons face severe challenges relating to access, inclusion, discrimination, empowerment, and equality. In an attempt to address this, the government of Jamaica has launched several initiatives to facilitate the inclusion of people with disability in social and economic life as well as political life.

The Jamaica Council for Persons with Disabilities (JCPD) is the government's institution with responsibility to implement and monitor policies and programmes for people with disabilities in Jamaica. In addition to recent legislation, the Jamaican Constitution guarantees all citizens, including the disabled, the right to participate in the democratic space. Several civil society institutions such as Jamaica Society for the Blind, Jamaica Society for the Deaf, Jamaica Association for Children with Learning Disabilities (JACLD), Jamaica Association for Children with Mental Retardation (JACMR), Abilities Foundation, Private Voluntary Organizations Ltd. (PVO), 3D Projects, Combined Disabilities Association (CDA), the Jamaica Council for Persons with Disabilities and the Council for Voluntary Social Services (CVSS) have been instrumental in addressing discrimination against the disabled, fostering access, promoting empowerment, inclusion, and equality. For the most part, the outcome for many disabled people has been positive. In the last decade, much work has been done to include the disabled in the Jamaican social life. For example, many important televised events are broadcast using sign language interpretation, and most institutions have had to provide accessibility to persons in wheelchairs.

Considerable work has done in the last two decades to address the needs of the visually and hearing impaired. For example, in 2000 the government of Jamaica implemented the National Policy for Persons with Disabilities which 'advocates the principles of equality and non-discrimination against persons with disabilities in areas such as education and training, housing and family life, and accessibility.' Additionally, Vision 2030, a document developed to guide Jamaica into achieving developed country status by 2030, outlines several initiatives to enhance the well-being of this group.

As will be discussed in chapters 5 and 6, despite previously mentioned policies and achievements, to date there has only been one visually impaired citizen that has held public office. The reality is that accessing, interacting with, and processing information are still barriers for the blind, and communication is still a barrier for the hearing impaired. Additionally, discrimination and lack of awareness on the part of the wider society are also barriers to participation. Persons with disabilities have a right to vote and to exercise their democratic rights at all levels in the decision-making process but they do not always get the opportunity do so.

Barbados

Barbados has a population of just over 280,000, of which approximately 12,000 are disabled. Though there are no laws in Barbados which prohibit discrimination against people with disability or seek to encourage equality, participation, and/or inclusion of disabled persons, the Barbados Constitution does contain anti-discrimination provisions. Barbados too is a signatory to the Convention which provides guidelines for governments to address the challenges of the disabled in their countries. In addition to the Convention, there have been local discussions about disability which have led to a White Paper on Persons with Disability that was approved by the Barbadian Parliament in 2002 and revised in 2009. Most of the government's activities related to disability issues are implemented and monitored by the National Disabilities Unit of the Ministry of Social Care. In addition to this Unit, various ministries have been doing fairly good work in addressing issues of accessibility and inclusion as well as empowerment (Barbados Government Information Service 2007).

The Barbados Council for the Disabled is a civil society organization that has helped to significantly shape the direction of disability issues in Barbados. The Council has spearheaded a number of projects and initiatives and has provided guidelines for other organizations interested in doing disability work. Despite the efforts of the government and civil society, there is still much work that needs to be done in Barbados.

Conclusion

People with disabilities face several challenges in many parts of the world. Since 2000, there have been many initiatives at the global and local levels that have helped to address these challenges such as accessibility, inclusion, and empowerment. Though there have been many success stories, particularly in relation to the livelihood of people with disabilities and including them in social life, not enough has been done specifically relating to their inclusion in the democratic and political life of countries around the world. This is evidenced by the very small number of disabled persons in representative politics as well as the number of disabled persons participating in the electoral process. The following chapter explores the issues specifically relating to the disabled occupying the democratic space in the Caribbean and is based on interviews with persons with disability in Jamaica and Barbados.

Chapter 4
Assistive Technology
– A History of Technology and People with Disabilities

There has always been some level of ambivalence between disabled persons and the rest of society. On the one hand, disabled persons rely on and appreciate the assistance of others in dealing with their handicaps. On the other hand, they often feel marginalized by society because of their handicaps. This is often seen as making life harder for disabled persons because it increases their sense of powerlessness and dependence. One way of bridging this chasm is the development of tools, which would enhance the personal skills of disabled persons in order for them to be included in society and escape the personal and social trap, as well as encourage participation in political, social, and economic spaces. This chapter explores some of these technological tools.

Assistive Technologies (ATs)

'Assistive technologies' (ATs) is the term used to describe any product or service that seeks to maintain or improve the ability of individuals with disabilities or impairments to communicate, learn, and live independent, fulfilling, and productive lives. D. Cowan and A. Turner-Smith (1999, 325) define it as 'an umbrella term for any device or system that allows an individual to perform a task they would otherwise be unable to do or increases the ease and safety with which the task can be performed.' Examples of ATs are screen reader software which provide an aural translation of the information on the screen; voice recognition software which allows people to navigate with voice rather than a keyboard or mouse, and many input devices such as large keyboards and mouse pedals.

It is highly probable that assistive technology for the disabled dates back to prehistoric times. 'As soon as primitive humans fashioned clubs and axes to facilitate hunting and gathering, others must have designed crutches and canes to compensate for physical handicaps' (Coombs 1990, 1).

1900s to the 1950s

The modern day representation of assistive technologies dates back to the 1500s with the works of Girolama Cardano (1501–1576), an Italian physician, philosopher and mathematician who wrote in *De Subtilitate* about how sound may be transmitted to the ear by means of a rod or the shaft of a spear held between one's teeth (Washington Univesrsity School of Medicine 2009) and others such as the Spanish monk, Pedro Ponce de Leon (1520–84); the Italian physician, scientist, and cryptographer Giovanni Battista Porta (1535–1615); the German scholar, mathematician, and philosopher Athanasius Kircher (1602–80); the paraplegic watchmaker Stephen Farfler (1633–89) who built the self-propelling chair on a three wheel chassis (the first wheel chair); and the development of the funnel or conical ear trumpets (hearing devices) such as the Townsend Trumpet, the Reynolds Trumpet (designed for British portrait painter Joshua Reynolds), and the Daubeney Trumpet, to name a few. The development of the Bath wheelchair in 1783 in Bath, England and the Audiphone bone conduction amplifier at the end of the 18th century are the defining moments in ATs. The Audiphone bone conduction amplifier was an early bone conduction hearing aid device recognized as the earliest form of hearing aid. Hearing was amplified through the conduction of sound through bone.

The 19th century saw the development of the typewriter and the telephone, which were regarded as critical technologies that aided persons with disabilities. These devices were initially developed to assist people with disabilities but became mainstream as time progressed. Interestingly, the first portable electronic hearing aid was developed using telephone technology (Sandlin 2000). By 1902, the first commercial hearing aid was developed in the United States of America (USA) by Miller Reese Hutchinson. This was referred to as the *Akouphone*, which was a miniaturized hearing aid.

In 1892, the first brailler machine was invented by Frank Hall. This was based on work done earlier by Louis Braille in the 1820s. Braille is a tactile writing system of raised dots which allows individuals to read by running their fingers along the dots and can be used to both read and write. Frank Hall's brailler was an improvement of Louis Braille's invention and other braillers which were invented thereafter. By the early 1900s, handmade brailler machines similar to Hall's design were built at the Perkins School for the Blind in the US. These were further improved upon.

In the 1920s, radios began finding their way into homes and in 1928, the American Foundation for the Blind distributed radios to provide blind persons with access to information that previously was only available in print formats. By 1934, the Readphone was invented which reproduced literature and music on discs. This was a very useful device for blind persons. The following year, with developments in the recording industry, talking books were created following the invention of Thomas Edison's phonograph, which allowed the production and use of talking books for the blind.

In 1936, the first speech synthesizer was invented. It was called VODER (Voice Operating Demonstrator) and was inspired by VOCODER (Voice Coder) initially developed at Bell Laboratories in 1928. According to Sami Lemmetty (1999), 'the original VOCODER was a device for analysing speech into slowly varying acoustic parameters that could then drive a synthesizer to reconstruct the approximation of the original speech signal' (Lemmetty 1999, 6). VODER paved the way for the invention of both text-to-speech and speech-to-text technologies.

In 1941, the prototype of Perkins Brailler, a more advanced brailler, was developed by David Abraham, but it was not actually produced until after the Second World War in 1951. This prototype advanced the earlier invention of Braille by Louis Braille in the 1820s. This tactile writing system of raised dots was a breakthrough for people who are blind, because, unlike earlier embossed-letter reading systems, Braille can be used to both read and write (Seymour-Ford 2009).

Perkins' design was revolutionary because it was lightweight, quiet, and far less prone to breakage than the previous type of Braille machine.

The 1940s saw significant advances in hearing aid technologies, for hearing impaired individuals. By 1948, the first transistor hearing aids were pioneered by Bell Laboratories. Miniaturized hearing aids were developed and considerably contributed to the lives of hearing impaired individuals by enhancing their quality of life.

The period also saw the evolution of the wheelchair with the development of the motorized wheelchair in 1916. Later in 1932, Harry Jennings, an engineer, built the first folding tabular steel wheelchair, which is similar to what is in modern use.

1960s to the 2000s

There were radical development of ATs during the 1960s as well. Canadian George Klein, with the help of the National Research Council of Canada, developed the electric wheelchair. Additionally, the first full English text-to-speech synthesis was developed by Noriko Umeda at the Electrotechnical Laboratory in Japan, based on earlier work in the late 1950s. It was based on an articulatory model and included a syntactic analysis module with sophisticated heuristics. The speech was quite intelligible but monotonous and far away from the quality of present systems (Klatt 1987). A decade later, the first handheld device with speech synthesizer was developed.

In 1976, Ray Kurzweil invented the first Kurzweil Reading Machine. This reading software advanced the understanding of omni-font optical character recognition (OCR) and flatbed scanner technology. Kurzweil connected those technologies to a text-to-speech synthesizer to produce the reading machine.

In 1982, Drs Jim and Janet Baker founded Dragon Systems based on early speech synthesizing technology. Ten years later in 1992, computer operating systems began including speech synthesizers in computer text-to-speech programmes to help people with reading disabilities and/or visual impairments access written material. In 1996, two decades after its inception, the Kurzweil Educational Systems, in 1996, began providing text-to-speech capability to allow persons with visual impairment or reading disability to access any print material using scanner technology while highlighting the text being read.

The Next Generation of Assistive Technologies

The twenty-first century ushered in a new generation of ATs. In 2006, the National Federation of the Blind (NFB), an organization of blind people in the US, unveiled a groundbreaking new device, the Kurzweil–National Federation of the Blind Reader. This portable reader, developed by renowned inventor Ray Kurzweil, enables users to take pictures of and read most printed materials at the click of a button (National Federation of the Blind 2006). The Next Generation Perkins Brailler was released in February 2008, reconfigured for the 21st century. Shortly thereafter, in 2012, the Perkins Smart Brailler – a fully digitalized brailler – was introduced. It was the first truly digital brailler, which allows people with visual impairments to participate in the digital world. This device has USB interface and text-to-speech capability along with the typical Braille interface. With this new Braille, a person with visual impairments does not have to learn the analogue version of Braille to manipulate written documents. The introduction of computer hardware and software in particular by companies such as Apple and Microsoft both of which have developed applications for persons with special needs, have also advanced the availability of ATs.

The future for ATs is very promising because 'as technology moves forward, dead ends that previously seemed to block advancement can be circumnavigated to find new solutions – even ones that previously seemed impossible,' (Willis 2015). The introduction of wireless technology and Bluetooth, in particular, has made the future even more promising as it allows for greater connectivity for persons of all abilities. More applications,

Braille mobile phones, and tablets as well as vision-correcting software offer vast potential for transforming the lives of visually impaired persons.

Now

Information and Communication Technologies as Assistive Technologies

There is a growing body of research which suggests that access to ICTs leads to significant improvement in the life of persons suffering from disabilities and that those without access are being functionally excluded from the mainstream society (Florian and Hegarty 2004; International Telecommunications Union 2013; Istenic Starcic and Bagon 2014; Koutkias et al. 2016). This has created a new mindset where assistance given to people with disabilities has moved away from the realm of charity and more towards being considered an obligation, a fundamental human right. Since many disabilities make it difficult, if not impossible, for persons to move around freely and without much assistance, being able to maintain societal interaction from home and/or in adapted environments is an extremely liberating and empowering experience.

The Internet is type of ICT which is a medium where many people with disabilities can interact to pursue interests, conduct business, acquire information, partake in education and training, get healthcare information, engage in employment activities, be entertained and keep up to date with the news (Florian and Hegarty 2004; Istenic Starcic and Bagon 2014; Koutkias et al. 2016; International Telecommunications Union 2013). Persons who deal with immobility can shop online and have their groceries and other products delivered. Government information and services can be accessed online through e-government. One of the main advantages is that all this information is brought to the user, without the need for much physical movement or relocation. With ICTs, users, even those with some disabilities, are able to navigate their social and physical environments as well as take more command of their prospects and future. This provides them with increased opportunity to earn a living as well as to be more involved in aspects of government, politics, civil society, and other decision-making processes. Several governments and civil society groups now endorse and practise making their websites more accessible to persons with disabilities by providing computer kiosks in communities, through computer donation programmes, and employing ICTs in schools.

Accessibility refers not only to having access to the technology to get online, but also being able to utilize it in a useful way. Through computers, smartphones, digital television, and tablets, information is constantly at our fingertips. Many of these devices have to be retrofitted to be accessible by persons with certain motor and physical challenges and disabilities. Blind people are able to read what is on the screen through screen readers that read the text aloud. Deaf persons are able to keep up with live events through online real time sources and closed-captioning that updates with text; something that was once only available through the radio or on television. Other physical disabilities such as the effects of polio and multiple sclerosis may require the user to use headsticks to interact with a screen or may affect their ability to use a mouse to control a cursor. In these cases, physical and technical interventions hold the solutions to getting persons on a computer and logging in online.

Browser accessibility is also a major tool where being able to resize the text and images on web pages, as well as turning off background images and changing the text and background colours on pages, helps many persons with visual and cognitive disabilities. Many of these features also benefit persons with low literacy, low bandwidth, and new users to the Internet, thereby widening the net of beneficiaries.

Microsoft, one of the world's most popular software companies, has integrated speech recognition into its operating systems, the Windows Vista program, allowing persons to use their computer with no arms or hands at no added cost. Apple has also added VoiceOver screen reader into its iOS and MacOS operating systems to help visually challenged persons, and IBM has strongly pushed for the Accessible Rich Internet Applications standard all over the world. The Kinect attachment for the Xbox and the PC is also a great assistive device for persons with autism.

Governments across the world are also playing their role in the use of ICTs to promote the inclusion of PWDs in social, economic, and in some instances of public life. Around the globe, nations have adopted their own initiatives to help mainstream persons with disabilities. These initiatives range from the donation of free equipment in the US to the provision of computer-based assistive technology being used in schools across the US. Hong Kong, Canada, and Australia are well advanced in enhancing their government websites for people with disabilities. This action on the part of these governments allows persons with disabilities to access important information. In South Africa, a National Accessibility Programme synthesizes data and provides a communication service that is meant to assist persons with disabilities as a one-stop-shop for various services and products. Through the online portal, persons are able to find caregivers, view job openings and apply for employment, and solicit government services. It was an answer to the prohibitively expensive nature of common assistive ICT services and is now a model for the entire African continent.

The importance of ICTs to the lives of PWDs is also recognized by international organizations and international foundations as well. In 2001, the United Nations Ad Hoc Committee on the Comprehensive and Integral Convention on the Protection and Promotion of the Rights and Dignity of Persons with Disabilities was formed, and on March 30, 2007, the Convention on the Rights of Persons with Disabilities (CRPD) was opened for signature. It came in force on May 3, 2008. Prior to this, there was the Standard Rules on the Equalization of Opportunities for Persons with Disabilities (1994) and the World Programme of Action on Disabled Persons (1982) neither of which were legally binding. The general principles of the CRPD are outlined in Article 3 which speaks to the deserved respect for persons with disabilities to make their own choices, to be free of discrimination, and have full participation in society. The principles also instruct that persons with disabilities receive equal opportunity and accessibility. The document makes particular note of the role of ICTs in Article 9 as a tool to help disabled persons live independently and participate in all aspects of society.

The CRPD implores governments to develop guidelines on how public facilities can be made available and accessible to persons with disabilities. The goal is to provide the same quality of service to all persons and so it includes the proper use of ramps, signage in Braille, and captioning on public television. It also speaks to the use of e-government under Article 9.2 and makes specific recommendations for electronic voting through electronic kiosks. Many countries and international organizations have been motivated by the CPRD and so in the last decade, there has been a plethora of activity at the international level geared towards promoting the use of ICTs to encourage PWDs to participate in public, social, and economic life.

In 2013 for example, the International Telecommunication Union (ITU) published 'The ICT Opportunity for a Disability-Inclusive Development Framework: Synthesis report of the ICT Consultation in support of the High-Level Meeting on Disability and Development of the sixty-eighth session of the United Nations General Assembly'. This hallmark document represented an attempt to highlight the importance of improving access to ICTs for persons with disabilities to enhance their inclusion in mainstream society. The report was the product of a series of consultations with 150 experts from around the world. One of the key report findings was the contribution of web services (and the associated technologies used to access these web services particularly mobile phones) to promoting the inclusion of people with disability. This is depicted in figure 4.1.

According to the ITU, the computer/Internet and associated software applications allow users to participate in several aspects of social, economic, and political life. The Internet provides opportunities for people with disabilities for social participation such as social networking, accessing the news, accessing government websites, and connecting with agents of the state (ITU 2013). The report stated:

For persons with disabilities, these services and content are made further accessible through both computer-based and web-based accessibility applications such as screen readers, speech recognition, video communication (for sign language communication and video relay interpretation), voice to text services (open and closed captioning, both real time and embedded) and visual assistance....Websites can provide visual, audio and text output on demand and offer multimedia input opportunities to users, making traditional unifunctional radio and schedule-driven traditional TV broadcasting technologies increasingly irrelevant (ITU 2013, 8–9).

One example of the significance of ICTs such as computer/Internet to people with disabilities was articulated by Anriette Esterhuysen, Executive Director, Association for Progressive Communications (APC) in the report. She stated:

The Internet has acted as a platform for collaboration for all types of organisations. It has allowed for all citizens, including people with disabilities, to engage more actively in political and social life. The Internet in itself could be considered an assistive technology, allowing voices to be heard that traditionally could not be (Anriette Esterhuysen quoted in the International Telecommunications Union 2013, 9).

In addition to the computer/Internet, the mobile phone was also identified as being of contributive value to people with disabilities, even more substantive than the computer/Internet because of their portability, ease of access, and in some instances, cost. Smartphones in particular:

...address the unique sensory, physical and cognitive needs of customers with disabilities. A variety of smartphones are rated for hearing aid compatibility. Customers can enjoy open or closed-captioned multimedia content and use face-to-face video chat applications or dedicated video relay services to communicate via sign language. They are also able to access content non-visually through screen reading applications, customize alert settings to use a combination of audible, visual, and vibration alerts and take advantage of voice-commands, adjustable font sizes, predictive text and a range of other innovative features, accessories, and third party applications (ITU 2013, 11).

Figure 4.1: Expert Assessment of the Contribution of ICTs to Improving Persons with Disabilities' Access to Social and Economic Activities

4.0–5.0: **To a large extent** 3.0–3.9: **To a moderate extent** 2.0–2.9: **To some extent** 1.0–1.9: **To little extent** 0.0–0.9: **Not at all**	Websites	Mobile device & services	Traditional TV set & services	Traditional Radio	Other & emerging technologies	ICTs most impactful where?
Healthcare	3.3	3.1	2.9	2.5	2.7	2.9
Primary education	3.0	2.6	2.8	2.3	2.9	2.7
Secondary education	3.4	3.0	2.7	2.3	2.8	2.8
Tertiary, professional, lifelong education	3.7	3.4	2.9	2.4	2.8	3.0
Employment	3.7	3.3	2.5	2.2	2.7	2.8
Independent living	3.4	4.6	2.8	2.4	2.8	3.2
Government services	3.5	3.0	3.0	2.3	2.6	2.8
Participation in political & public life	3.3	3.1	2.7	2.5	2.6	2.8
Overall average	3.4	3.2	2.7	2.3	2.7	

Source: Authors, based on the results of the ICT consultation

Source: ITU, 2013

Figure 4.2 depicts the composition of these ICTs that can contribute to the inclusion of people with disabilities.

Figure 4.2: Impactful Technologies

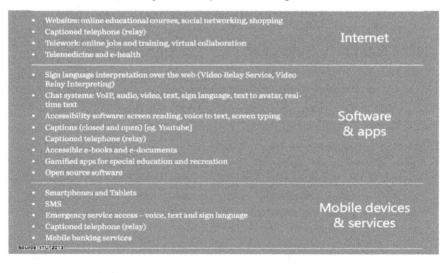

Source: ITU, 2013

The World Bank has ensured that its communication network is accessible and performs special work on raising awareness on the issue through sponsoring and staging conferences, consultations, and using language that promotes inclusion. A recent background paper for the 2016 World Development Report: entitled 'Digital Dividends: Bridging the Disability Divide through Digital Technologies' by Deepti Samant Raja of the World Bank Group recognized the importance of ICTs for PWDs and sought to 'provide an overview of the opportunities presented by the Internet and ICT for the full participation of persons with disabilities' (Raja 2016). According to Raja (2016):

> The exclusion and marginalization of persons with disabilities is a human rights issue as well as an economic issue for countries. When a significant section of society, estimated at 15 percent of the world's population, faces obstacles in receiving an education, transitioning into the labor market, and becoming economically self-sufficient, it not only undermines their rights and dignity but adds significantly to a country's welfare burden (WHO and World Bank 2011). Information and Communication Technology (ICT) is increasingly enabling persons with disabilities to level the playing field in access to lifelong education, skills development, and employment (Broadband Commission for Digital Development et al. 2013). The confluence of two major trends is reshaping the paradigm on using technology to promote inclusion and full participation of persons with disabilities.

> The first is that the Internet and Information and Communication Technology (ICT) are becoming common and popular channels for the delivery and implementation of governance, welfare, socioeconomic development, and human rights programming (Samant, Matter, and Harniss 2012). They are transforming pathways to poverty reduction by enabling direct interactions between producers and markets globally, new methods of delivering personalized public and social services quickly, different channels for income generation, and innovations in asset accumulation and access to finance....The internet also enables multiple channels to access and contribute information, with a global reach, which can improve transparency, accountability, and monitoring of development programs and services. Multiple delivery channels are being used for communication and service delivery including email, text messaging, voice communications, and video.

> The second is that a growing number of mainstream, everyday ICT such as mobile devices and desktop computers increasingly offer functionalities that facilitate communication and information access for persons with disabilities. Features such as text-to-speech and voice recognition, ability to change contrast and color schemes, touch and gesture input, and screen

magnification which in the past required specialized standalone software and hardware are embedded within off-the-shelf ICT devices.

Digital technologies enable persons with disabilities to receive information and content in the format that they can perceive and prefer. For example, a person with visual impairments can use speech-to-text functionality or software to read a website, a person with hearing impairments can use SMS or instant text messaging to communicate, and a person with mobility impairments can use voice recognition to operate and navigate their digital device.

This presents an important opportunity to break the traditional barriers of communication and interaction that persons with disabilities face and which hinder their full participation in society.

A recent survey of 150 experts from over 55 countries ranked websites and mobile devices and services as the technologies that can contribute the most to the social and economic inclusion of persons with disabilities.... The experts also perceived the highest impact of ICT for individuals with disabilities to be on independent living, employment, education, and access to government services (Raja 2016).

This is, however, not just rhetoric, as there is increasing recognition and actual evidence that ICTs can have a positive impact on the democratic landscape in many ways. The introduction of e-voting, for example, provides the possibility of voting from home or wherever one has access to the Internet. While electronic voting has been around for decades, the introduction of remote electronic voting has new possibilities for including more persons in the process, especially those suffering from the most challenging disabilities. Not only can persons stay at home and vote, but also there are increased possibilities for the ballot to be made more accessible and user friendly.

In Canada, the federal government has used e-consultations as a way to facilitate the inclusion of opinions of persons from all over including those with disabilities. In these cases, online forums are created to run for a set period of time so as to collect information from the public regarding a particular issue that the government is contemplating. Persons are allowed to log on to the forum and share stories, offer solutions, and partake in polling. According to Deborah Stienstra and Lindsey Troschuk (2005), while these forums have a lot of potential, governments need to ensure that there are set guidelines and standards in their design and that there is a proactive strategy to enlist participation. The language on the site must also be plain and clear for persons with development disabilities to understand.

It has been recognized that 'the advancements in technology are insufficient by themselves to bridge the gaps in the socioeconomic inclusion of persons with disabilities' (Raja 2016, 4). Accordingly:

The adaptation, operationalization, and implementation of ICT for inclusive development remains dependent on others factors within the ecosystem.... Existing evidence shows that the success of using the internet and ICT for the inclusion of persons with disabilities is heavily impacted by stakeholders' knowledge and awareness of the ICT solutions available, laws and policies, and the capacity of various stakeholders to support accessible ICT services.... In fact, the use of the Internet and ICT can widen the disparities between persons with and without disabilities if they are not designed to be accessible and inclusive (Raja 2016).

The World Bank recognizes that though ICTs have the potential to enhance access for PWDs, they can also contribute to creating barriers for them as well. One such barrier is the digital divide.

The digital divide is a term used to refer to a state of unequal access to digital technology within or between countries; the gap between those who have access to ICTs/ICT infrastructure as well as the availability of ICTs/ICT infrastructure, and those who do not. The digital divide is also a function of awareness, access, knowledge, information, education and capacity. As mentioned in previous chapters, PWDs face severe economic and social barriers. Access to technologies has recently been recognized as one of them. In a world where technologies are becoming a normal means of engagement, empowerment, and enterprise, being unable to access such technologies, being unaware of these technologies and not having the capacity to use these technologies can have an even greater impact on PWDs.

According to the World Bank (2016), persons living with a disability account for approximately 15.3 per cent of the world's population. This equates to one billion people. Eighty per cent of them live in rural areas in developing countries and about 186 million are unable to complete primary school education. The unemployment rate for the disabled is 70 per cent in developed countries and 90 per cent in developing countries, placing them at a serious disadvantage of being able to earn and support their families. Other statistics confirm the gap, with the probability of regularly using a computer, or Internet access dropping for persons with a disability. The issue is therefore twofold – getting persons with a disability to access the technology as well as removing the virtual and physical barriers that exist once they have access to ICT resources.

In poorer countries, illiteracy is one of the major challenges to using ICTs. Telecommunication infrastructure is also an issue where poor access to computers, low Internet penetration, and low bandwidth affect the ability for ICT to be of real assistance. Since people with disabilities generally have lower income and less education than the general public, they are already at a disadvantage and are more likely to suffer from these problems. Laurent Elder et al. (2013) place the issue in a broader context noting that the approach has to be a social one, not just technical in nature. Unfortunately, in today's information society, ICTs' role in aiding persons with disabilities is still considered to be a peripheral thought rather than at the core of development.

It is clear that persons with disabilities are often natural victims of access. Most technologies such as ICTs are not usually made for persons with disabilities. And though software and hardware manufacturers do include components to address some disabilities, they cannot address them all. According to J. Simpson (2009), information and communication technologies must be designed, developed, and fabricated at the outset for accessibility and usability for people with disabilities. She further argues:

> Absent this design and development approach, people with disabilities are left behind and are forced to play catch-up — an expensive and undesirable path. It is important to note that no matter what the stage of development of the communications infrastructures — such as wire line or broadband or wireless networks or the television delivery infrastructure — disability advocates and interested others can work to ensure that barriers are removed or, just as importantly, are not created as technology infrastructures advance (Simpson 2009, 1).

Indeed, persons who live with disabilities are considered to be some of the most disadvantaged people operating in the modern society, because of the virtual and physical barriers they face to accessing and utilizing products, services, and information that are not designed to fit their abilities. The general consensus, however, is that while there are challenges in the new digital age, the technology also provides new opportunities to help bridge the gap between persons who suffer from disabilities and those who do not. This is rooted in the development of assistive technology and the proper application of existing technology, along with changes in the method of content provision to more suit the needs of everyone.

Many services and products are still out of reach because other obstacles remain on many websites that are not designed to accommodate the needs of people with certain disabilities or are incompatible with the assistive technologies that they use. Software developers and manufacturers have yet to fully include the needs of persons with disabilities despite the global thrust to do so.

Conclusion

The potential for ICT to include persons with disabilities in mainstream society and governmental decision-making is increasingly being recognized the globe over. However, ICT has not been fully utilized and employed to its maximum benefit. The 2012–2013 CRPD progress report noted there were some critical success factors contributing to making the ratification of the Convention more effective. These included: the existence of a government body with specific responsibility for addressing the needs of persons with disabilities; a systematic mechanism to design and produce a legal framework that will be used to set accessibility standards; financial support for bodies that assist with aiding persons with disabilities; forums for persons working in the field of aiding persons with disabilities so they may cooperate; awareness programmes and laws that promote training in the area, and; country participation in helping to set international guidelines and standards. There is also a significant opportunity to target infrastructure service providers like telephone companies to have greater impact on the population.

ICTs generally, and e-Democracy specifically, should be viewed as a way of strengthening the democracy in any country. Online participation and public services open a door to many people who were previously excluded from the process. However, there is still a need for more research to be done on who exactly are using these services and to know what the real impact is. Indeed this book will contribute to that knowledge base.

Chapter 5
'Knowledge' and 'Talk'
but No 'Inclusion' and No 'Equity'

Introduction

This chapter highlights the experiences of visually impaired citizens in Jamaica and Barbados particularly in relation to their participation in the democratic space. The findings from several interviews that were conducted with visually impaired individuals in these countries are presented and for comparative purposes, the chapter also draws on literature capturing the experiences of persons who are visually impaired in North America, Europe, New Zealand, as well as parts of Africa, Asia, and Latin America. More specifically, the chapter focuses on how and in what ways Information and Communication Technologies (ICTs) have contributed to the lives of visually impaired citizens in these countries, particularly in accessing the democratic space.

The data analysed suggests that ICTs have substantively contributed to the lives of many (but certainly not all) visually impaired persons in various ways by improving their political knowledge (or awareness about different aspects of politics) and promoting political talk (talking about politics). Despite these developments, some visually impaired persons feel excluded in the democratic space. Two of the four research questions which guided this study posed are answered in this chapter. Firstly, what has been the experience of visually impaired citizens using ICTs to facilitate their access and participate in the democratic space? And secondly, to what extent have ICTs addressed the challenges of equity and inclusion faced by visually impaired Caribbean citizens?

ICT and Political Knowledge

The enhancement of political knowledge was identified by those interviewed for this study, as one of the ways in which ICTs aided visually impaired Caribbean citizens to be included in the democratic space. Historically, it has been well established that an informed (and thus knowledgeable) citizenry contributes to a stable democracy (Easton 1965; 1975; Moon 1990; Delli Carpini and Keeter 1993; 1996; Andersen, Heath, and Sinnot 2001; 2002; Dalton 2004) or at the very least, 'the quality of democratic representation and accountability of office holders' (Milner

2008, 3). K. Grönlund and H. Milner (2006) explain this in some more detail:

> Democratic theorists from John Stuart Mill to Robert Dahl have stressed the importance of political information in democratic decision-making. Since representative democracy is based on the delegation of power from citizens to representatives, the defining moment is at the time of elections: for democracy to function properly, electors need to have sufficient knowledge of the political system and the political actors in order to cast a meaningful vote. If they are to ensure that political parties and leaders are accountable for their actions, voters need information to evaluate their performance. They need to be able to compare parties' commitments and manifestos in a prospective manner against their own political preferences and, in retrospect, to know enough about the parties' record to give some weight to the credibility of their commitments (386).

Citizens, many argue, should possess at least some understanding of the 'political system through which [at the very least] they express their preferences and elect their representatives' (Memoli 2011, 85). Citizens should be aware of their system of government and the process of governance. A knowledgeable and informed citizenry is therefore a prerequisite for ensuring that the citizens are able to articulate how they are governed, how decisions are made and implemented, ensure that their fundamental rights and freedoms are respected, can hold their leaders accountable –ensuring that governments are responsible, responsive, efficient, effective, transparent, and accountable, and are being respectful of international norms and principles. This is referred to as 'political knowledge'.

Political knowledge is broadly defined here as 'factual information held by members of the public' (Oxley 2012, 27). This definition is preferred as it captures the varied popular representations of political knowledge in the literature (see, for example, Prior 2007; Delli Carpini and Keeter 1996). M.X. Delli Carpini and S. Keeter (1996) identified three types of political knowledge: (1) The rules of the game – the focus on the structure of government such as the duties of each branch of government; (2) The substance of politics – what the critical issues are, their history, relevance, and alternatives, and (3) The people and players in politics –awareness of the current leaders of a country and other nations as well as these leaders and important political groups.

Conversely, the lack of political knowledge or lack of trust in particular sources of political knowledge can be detrimental to the well-being of a democracy. It can have harmful effects such as 'ill-informed voting choices, inability to articulate political interests, and a lack of ability to hold political leaders accountable'(Varela 2010; see also Nicholson, Pantoja, and Segura 2006). It can also produce a lack of awareness about harmful public and international policies, as well as decisions, attitudes, actions, and perceptions. Additionally, lack of political knowledge can induce a state of political apathy, discourage political participation and political talk. All this has wider implications for undermining democracy, and in particular, good governance. Indeed, political knowledge depends on the availability of free information provided by the context, and in particular, by the media, which are the main sources of political information for citizens (Anduiza, Gallego, and Jorba 2012).

The literature identifies several sources of political knowledge. These include the family, the education system, groups, and the media. Modern conversations about the media recognize both traditional and digital media. Whereas traditional media represents radio, television, and print media, digital media represents the media accessed through digital means such as the Internet (social media, blogs, websites etc.).

Interestingly, none of the participants interviewed believed that their disability limited their interest in Jamaican or Barbadian politics. Most of the visually impaired persons engaged had a keen interest in politics especially Jamaican or Barbadian politics. Indeed, there was a strong conviction about the importance of politics in their respective countries. Two examples are presented below of two visually impaired youth interviewed for the study:

> Politics is something that we Caribbean people love. It is in our blood. It does not matter if we are blind or deaf we just love politics. We eat drink and sleep politics. We love to discuss politics when we lyme (talk among each other), we speak politics in the classroom and at work.... Being blind does not mean that you are unaware of what happens around you. It is important that you know, that you have a say and that you are heard (Interviewee 15).

> Jamaican politics is something that you cannot escape from. It is everywhere. Regardless of the fact that you are blind or if you don't like politics you cannot escape it. You hear about it everywhere you go. Personally I love politics. I know that a lot of young people these days are not into politics. But this is bad. I think it has a lot to do with how certain persons in politics treat politics, the politicians. We cause it because we allow it to happen. Because we don't care. Well a lot of young people don't care. We are the ones who have to change the system....If I had the opportunity I would do so (Interviewee 4).

These voices articulated the sentiments of all the youth interviewed for this study. Another interviewee believed that all young people should be interested in the governance of their country. According to him and speaking specifically about Jamaica:

This is the country that help to shape our lives through social and economic programmes, so I believe we all should be interested. We all are stakeholders and we should all ensure that the development of our country is good. What we should do is to participate to hold our political officials accountable who we put in place to represent us (Interviewee 1).

The interviewees were familiar with issues surrounding the structure of government, such as, the duties of each branch of government and the electoral process. Additionally, most of the interviewees were able to answer the following questions: Do you know about Jamaican or Barbadian politics – certain issues, the main issues? How familiar are you with the three branches of government and how they operate in your country? How familiar are you with the electoral process? How much do you know about the politics of your country? What do you think are the main issues surrounding the politics of your country right now? How much do you know about the political parties in your country? How much do you know about the political leaders in your country as well as in other countries? Generally speaking, the source of political knowledge among the disabled was no different from their able-bodied counterparts. Their knowledge came from interaction at home, schools, groups, and traditional media, as well as the Internet.

Sources of Political Knowledge among the Disabled in the Caribbean

Knowledge about politics (rules, substance, people, and players) influences the level of attention citizens give to politics, their level of interest in politics, as well as how they apply and organize ideas about politics. Political knowledge can thus also be regarded as a form of political efficacy.

The Internet (Facebook, web pages, blogs, Twitter, and other online social networks) was identified as the primary source of political information by all the persons interviewed for this study. According to one interviewee, 'The Internet is the most beneficial tool for me, especially when it comes to sourcing information about politics whether locally, regionally, or internationally.' The interviewee further added, 'Whereas I am able to listen to the news on the television and the radio, the Internet provides me with wider access to information about politics, democracy and governance.' The interviewee further stated:

...unlike the radio and television which only provides information about current affairs and is limited in its local focus, except the foreign stations, the Internet allows me to search for information, to clarify terms and get definition so I am better able to understand the issues.

This access is facilitated through the use of a laptop, with the JAWS (Job Access with Speech) programme on my computer to read the online newspapers like the commentaries and columns [as well as] the letters that are written in both of the major newspapers. I am also affiliated with a political institution, so I'm au fait with happenings in the political arena.

The attraction to using the Internet was not surprising and is in keeping with global trends. The Internet allows users to access radio, newspapers, and television while at the same time providing a level of interactivity by allowing users to make comments and engage others. The Internet was usually accessible through a myriad of ICTs such as the mobile phone, a personal computer, a tablet or a notebook.

ICTs and Political Talk among the Visually Impaired

As discussed above, lack of political knowledge can induce a state of political apathy and discourage political participation and political talk. Based on the data analysed, beyond the use of ICTs to attain knowledge, the technologies were also used to facilitate political talk. Throughout history, political communication, and specifically 'political talk' has been seen as a form of democratic participation. Political talk is defined here as 'non-purposive, informal, casual, and spontaneous political conversation voluntarily carried out by free citizens, without being constrained by formal procedural rules and predetermined agenda' (Kim and Kim 2008, 53).

Seen as a critical component of political participation, which is a necessary precondition for good governance (Gastil 2000), political talk takes place at various levels of the political process (in privacy, among friends and family, or between elected representatives and citizens about political objects, subjects, events, processes, and phenomena). Political talk is increasingly viewed as a fundamental underpinning of economic development (Asen 2004; Delli Carpini, Cook, and Jacobs 2004; Gutmann and Thompson 1996; Neblo 2005; Duchesne and Haegel 2007).

Participation through political talk is interaction through talk/argument, text, or representation in music, other extra linguistic auditory signs between and among individuals or within a group operating in different networks, their elected representatives, or other affiliated actor(s) or institutions – and can be seen as public opinion. This interaction contributes to good governance either directly or indirectly. Occurring in homes, offices, churches, schools, and neighbourhoods, political talk can be discussions about social, economic, or political problems that groups, individuals, or an entire country face[s]. The process of talking about politics can also include proposals regarding solutions to these problems, attempts to persuade or win a debate/argument, concerns about what is being done, disadvantages and advantages about proposed solutions, and/or an attempt to understand these problems and related solutions. Benjamin Barber has concluded that 'everyday political talk undertakes the essential functions of a strong democracy' (1984, 54). Barber's position that 'conversation gives life to a notion of citizen' (184) is unassailable. A similar view was presented in the work by J. Kim and E.J. Kim (2008) who suggested that through everyday political talk citizens produce communicative reasons and achieve mutual understanding of self and others. Through everyday political talk, people now have an understanding of their own interests, what others want, and what fits the common good. Without this understanding, citizens may not be able to participate in instrumental deliberations in a meaningful way to make rational decisions (54).

Political talk also includes providing opportunities for 'ordinary citizens to construct the concept of the socio-political self in their daily lives' (Kim and Kim 2008, 58) and as the starting point for civic engagement and civic life. More recently, it has been used as a serious means of validation through online consultations on blogs or Online Social Networks (OSNs) such as Twitter and Facebook (De Zúñiga, Puig-I-Abril, and Rojas 2009).

Many of the interviewees articulated an interest in politics and more so stated that they frequently talked about politics online. Interviewee 1 for example, expressed a love for politics, which during the interview was represented by his constant conversations about many aspects of political life, not only with his family but also with his friends and colleagues in the lecture room at the University of the West Indies where he studies. He also interacts with total strangers online through Facebook where he engages in regular commentary on the politics of Jamaica through his posts, responds to comments about his posts, as well as other persons' comments. According to him, Facebook is a great avenue through which to express political ideas, and engage others about the politics of the day. He is able to read, engage, and participate sometimes using a mobile phone or some other handheld electronic device, or oftentimes through a computer or laptop and with the help of two screen readers: Non-Visual Desktop Access (NVDA) and Job Access with Speech (JAWS).

OSNs such as Facebook, Twitter, and even Instagram play a significant role in promoting political talk, particularly, among the youth. The Internet broadens the public sphere by providing the medium for extensive participation of people, especially youth in politics through a real-time, convenient, relatively cost-effective network. Essentially, this electronic network enables young people to talk politics online. OSNs have emerged as the new public sphere and a place for political talk and deliberation especially for the youth.

OSNs are virtual communities that allow 'individuals to present themselves to other users utilizing a variety of formats, including text and video' (Valenzuela, Park, and Kee 2009, 4). These communities are used for a myriad of purposes and activities. Some of the most popular activities include: making friends; posting status updates on one's profiles (sharing personal information, feelings, happenings etc.); posting comments, videos, and/or pictures on other persons' walls; linking other persons' status; sending messages to people; playing games or quizzes; posting links to events, news, or websites; inviting people (posting web links); creating events and extending invitations; creating groups for people (some of whom share common interest) to join as well as posting links to these events. According to Sebastian Valenzuela et al. (2009), young people around the world 'are motivated to join these sites to keep strong ties with friends, to strengthen ties with new acquaintances, and to a lesser degree, to meet new people online...(and to) exchange news and discuss issues' (1).

The specific contributive value of OSNs to visually impaired citizens is in affording them the opportunity to engage as citizens and not as *disabled* citizens. According to the interviewees, because they were located behind a screen, whether it was a PC, slate, tablet, or mobile screen, they were not treated differently in the way they say they normally are during face-to-face political talk. In the words of one interviewee, 'It makes us feel normal as if we belong. We are treated with respect, our voices are heard, and what we say is taken seriously' (Interviewee 8). She further stated:

> Sometimes when you talk about politics face-to-face with people, because you are blind, sometimes people don't take you seriously because there is this view you have no sense, like you don't know what you are saying because you have a disability. Once they see you with the disability their ratings (respect) for you goes down. So it is difficult for you to have a proper conversation with them (people without a disability). But when you are talking to them over the computer, on Facebook or Twitter or even by email you are treated differently, with some level of respect because the assumption is that you are normal like them and therefore you are intelligent (Interviewee 8).

Most of the interviewees shared a similar viewpoint. They generally agreed that ICTs aided them in their ability to not only talk about politics but also to allow the talk to be taken seriously.

The Power of ICTs and the Challenge of Inclusion and Equity among the Visually Impaired

Another theme which emerged was the fact that although ICTs have contributed to the ability of visually impaired Caribbean citizens to access and participate in the democratic space in terms of enhancing their knowledge and facilitating political talk for many of the participants, the technology did not do much to engender the *desired* type of inclusion and equity. Political inclusion and equity in the political processes of a country is a *sine-qua-non* of good governance and true democracy (Young 2002). Political inclusion and equity means that all members of society, particularly the most vulnerable, feel that their interests are accounted for and that they are provided with avenues by which to participate in the political processes within the democratic space. In other words, it means that they have a stake in a society. They are included, they are essentially then stakeholders. As illustrated in previous chapters, ICTs can encourage equity and inclusion particularly among minorities and vulnerable groups.

Though disabled, most of the persons interviewed believed that they have a stake in their society. One interviewee whose sentiments captured the viewpoint of those who believed they were stakeholders said, 'I believe I have a stake because I have access to the same information just as everybody else, so I don't think it is limited' (Interviewee 5). Those who shared this viewpoint believed that they are part of the democratic process, the democratic space, and that their disabilities do not in any way limit their ability to participate in the democratic and political space. According to one interviewee:

> I voted once...so that I don't think I have a limitation there and I'm participating within the governance by joining a political party and to put my suggestions forward as to how we can fast-track the developmental projects that would benefit Jamaica. So I don't believe that my disability is a hurdle in me participating in political affairs.

Not all interviewees, however, shared this view. For some, 'knowledge' and 'talk' did not translate into 'inclusion' nor 'equity'. These specific interviewees did not feel like they were fully a part of their respective country. They felt they had a voice but it was not heard. Those who felt excluded from mainstream society generally argue that visually impaired persons or persons with disabilities are not given equal opportunities in the same way that persons with sight have in mainstream society. This is particularly the case in relation to protesting, campaigning (participation), being able to monitor breach of accountability, and non-transparent actions of agents of the state or benefiting from government services (efficiency and effectiveness of government) like other visually abled citizens. They did not feel as though they were treated fairly and impartially. They also believe that they were generally excluded from these activities which are important social practices of citizenship. One of these participants who responded to the question, 'Do you believe that you have a stake in the Jamaican society or do you feel excluded from mainstream society?' explained:

> Well, there's a yes and no answer to that, in that, in order to access education there's no problem in accessing certain things such as education. However, in getting a job when you are actually fully trained that's where the difficulty actually comes in from time to time; you know because you are actually discriminated against you know. For example, I left the Mico Teachers College in 2009 and I went to several schools for interviews and I left these interviews feeling that I was being hard done by not being employed, in other words because I had a disability. You know it wasn't actually explicit but you could've detected that; 'hey you're not being employed here because you do have a disability. So it's a yes and no (Interviewee 2).

Other interviewees had similar stories:

> Sometimes I am excluded from some things like politics. Well as a group, persons with disabilities, would be what you call a minor group. So most of the time minority groups are ignored. People just respond to please you but they don't take you seriously. We get by but we don't get up and just like any minority group in the end we get left behind. One many occasions I have been overlooked for serious positions because of my disability and in many conversations my voice does not count because I am blind and therefore dumb (Interview 6).

> Well I do have a stake in terms of I do have a right but of course due to ignorance on the part of stakeholders and attempts have been made whether consciously or subconsciously to exclude the population of visually impaired or totally blind persons, or persons with disabilities in general from participating fully in the society. At least that has been the case where I am concerned as well as some of my other visually impaired friends (Interviewee 7).

Indeed, this was the view shared by at least eight of the 15 participants. That is, only being able to access some aspects of the Jamaican society and very few aspects of the democratic space. Accordingly, people with obvious disabilities, such as persons who are blind, 'are excluded from various national issues' (Interviewee 2). One of these persons who were interviewed cites an example:

For example, persons with hearing disabilities can't access news and other national information, as there are no sign language interpreters and persons with visual disabilities can't access some websites that the government has because the websites do not have up to date versions of screen-reading software, such as JAWS.

One Jamaican interviewee sought to explain the reason behind the treatment that they face generally and specifically as it relates to politics. According to the interviewee 'I do not think Jamaicans are educated enough, mature enough, to have persons with disabilities, especially a person who is visually impaired or blind take part in active politics. I don't think we're mature enough for that' (Interviewee 3). Indeed, this is one of the main challenges of the Jamaican education system (Cato 2011).

Conclusion

ICTs have contributed to the ability of visually impaired citizens in Jamaica and Barbados specifically by providing to access and facilitating participation in the democratic space in two specific ways. First, it provided another source of political knowledge for visually impaired Caribbean youth, a source other than traditional communications media. Second, it vastly expanded the scope of political talk for many of the participants (which is a form of political participation) among the visually impaired Caribbean youth interviewed for this study. This latter outcome was encouraged by the ability of ICTs to mask the disabilities of the participants behind a screen and thereby allowing them to be treated as equals and permitting their commentary on political issues to be taken more seriously. The study therefore suggests that to a great extent, ICTs have played a contributive role in terms of including the visually impaired Caribbean youth interviewed for this study in the democratic space.

The study validates emerging theoretical work which suggests that ICTs created immense opportunities for new forms of government–citizen communication, enable marginalized groups such as the disabled to participate in the democratic process (Roja 2016). Indeed, based on the findings of this study, ICTs have the potential to encourage visually impaired citizens, particularly the youth (who are more technologically engaged) to participate in democratic rituals such as political talk. Beyond its theoretical and empirical value, this study contributes to improving our understanding of how and in what ways ICTs can promote the inclusion of visually impaired persons in the democratic space and is valuable for individuals and institutions that implement and manage disability policies, projects and programmes for the visually impaired.

Chapter 6
Accessing the Political Spaces:
Challenges and Solutions

Introduction

The last chapter highlighted the experiences of visually impaired citizens in Jamaica and Barbados, particularly where it relates to their participation in the democratic space. Improving political knowledge and promoting political talk were identified as the two ways in which ICTs have aided visually impaired Caribbean citizens to access and participate in the democratic space. It was recognized, however, that despite the contributive value of ICTs, persons with visual impairment neither felt fully included in the democratic space of these countries nor did they feel any form of equity. This chapter explores the primary challenges that visually impaired Caribbean citizens face in using ICTs to access and participate in the democratic space. Solutions to these challenges are also explored. The chapter essentially answers the following research questions:

> What are the primary challenges that visually impaired Caribbean citizens experience with the use of ICTs to access and participate in the democratic space?

and

> Based on their experiences, what solutions do visually impaired Caribbean citizens offer to the challenges they face with the use of ICTs to access and participate in the democratic space?

Though the chapter focuses on the experiences of Caribbean citizens who are visually impaired, it can be of value to the global visually impaired citizenry as well as policymakers operating in government, international organizations, and civil society groups around the world who are keen to address inclusion and equity challenges faced by visually impaired citizens.

Equity in the Voting Process: Independent and Private Participation

Irrespective of the advancements in facilitating inclusion and equity, disability groups all over the world still do not feel that they are fully integrated in their respective societies (Lord, Stein, and Fiala-Butora 2014). As the previous chapter suggested, the Caribbean is no exception, although ICTs have been instrumental in terms of advancing the knowledge-base of visually impaired persons in Jamaica and Barbados. Many of these persons still feel isolated, excluded and inequitably treated in the democratic space. One particularly important concern in this regard, is voting.

While voting is not the sole determinant, it is most certainly a vital aspect of the democratic process and a core indicator of democratic maturity; indeed, no true democracy can exist without a fair and effective electoral moment (Schraufnagel and Sgouraki 2005). The literature identifies several reasons why voting is viewed as the most fundamental practice of political participation. The Weberian perspective stresses the importance of legitimate authority, guided by the rule of law (Orum and Dale 2008). The right to vote ensures that governments are legitimately appointed, reflecting the collective will of the people. Voting is also one of the ways that citizens can hold their elected leaders accountable along a number of dimensions including campaign promises (Johnson and Ryu 2010). Furthermore, it represents for citizens the opportunity to elect and re-elect the officials of the state, which has episodic and futuristic implication as it gives citizens the chance to contribute to policies at the local and national levels of government.

According to Deepti Samant Raja (2016) citing Lord, Stein, and Fiala-Butora (2014):

> The realization and exercise of human rights and citizenship is deeply intertwined with one's ability to participate in elections, engage in civic discourse, access governance, and obtain information on political and civic processes. Persons with disabilities have been deeply disenfranchised due to infrastructural barriers which impact their ability to engage in civic and electoral processes independently or privately (16).

There are many persons doing research on persons with disabilities (PWDs) who also share this view (See for example Lord, Stein, and Fiala-Butora 2014; Wildermuth 2006; Fiala-Butora, Stein, and Lord 2014). Therefore, not surprisingly, the visually and hearing impaired persons interviewed for this study were of the strong belief that much more needs to be done for the youths among them, particularly as it relates to the opportunity to independently participate in the voting process. There was recognition among the interviewees from both countries that 'the only time they really pay attention to the disabled persons is in the period of elections' (Interviewee 4). According to one interviewee, 'the need for votes was the reason why only during election time politicians really pay much attention to the disabled community... during this time, they go all out for us' (Interviewee 1). One interviewee described the rituals:

> So, they'll get their runners out to help the persons in the wheelchair go out and vote; the blind old man in the rural area; the deaf individuals and so on. They come to our houses and provide us with taxis to take us to the polling stations. They do everything for us. But because of our condition we sometimes don't want to participate, well not in the way they would want us to. We want to vote but independently. We want our independence and privacy (Interviewee 9).

The words 'independently', 'independent', and 'privacy' were common themes that emerged during conversations with the visually impaired persons interviewed for this study. Accordingly, because of their inability to see, visually impaired citizens in the countries under exploration as well as many other countries across the world are provided with support in the casting of ballots (Stein 1998; Alvarez, Atkeson, and Hall 2007; Lawson 2014). This support can either be provided by a close friend or family and/or (more likely) by an employee of the election commission. For many visually impaired citizens, this raises is a privacy concern. One interviewee opined, 'I believe at times our privacy has the potential to be eroded, so I believe to bring more privacy of our ballots and so on at elections' (Interviewee 1). According to another interviewee:

> ...as it stands the government does not allow the voting to meet the privacy needs of a person with visual disabilities. In order for a visual impaired person to vote, you have to have somebody sign the ballot paper for you and that in itself tarnish your privacy in voting in politics. So as soon as they get a system that's more garnered towards persons with visual disabilities such as Braille ballots and so forth, that's when visually impaired persons voting would be more in keeping with normal society (Interviewee 9).

Such concerns are valid and problematic for democracy globally. In the 2014 European and local elections, a survey of blind and partially sighted people conducted by the Royal National Institute of Blind People (RNIB) showed seven in ten visually impaired European voters had to give up their right to privacy. No study has been done in the Caribbean, however, based on the political culture of Caribbean societies it is not difficult to imagine a similar finding.

The need for voting privacy in the Caribbean political space is paramount. Many Caribbean countries have long been challenged by political victimization – unwarranted singling out of an individual or group because of their perceived political affiliation. Allegations, anecdotal accounts and representations of the fear of political victimization are well articulated in film, via the traditional media (television, radio, and print media) as well as social media (websites, blogs and social media). The articulation of the fear of political victimization is so prevalent that one could easily argue, as many in Jamaica have, that political victimization is a part of the political culture of Jamaican politics (Stone 1980; Sives 2002). This has contributed to a general fear, among many Caribbean citizens, of declaration of their political affiliation, and talking about politics (Stone 1980; National Committee on Political Tribalism 1997; Wantchekon 2003; Auyero 2000; Sives 2002; Edie 1989). Because of this possibility of victimization, many visually impaired persons who must rely on others to mark their ballots, tend to stay away from the polling stations. They are turned off because of a combination of this issue of privacy and the fear of victimization (Waller 2013).

The declining participation in what is often considered as the most fundamental democratic practice, has been viewed by many as a crisis in democracy and by others as a possible threat to the sustainability or legitimization of democracy and part of a larger 'democratic deficit' (Bennett 2008; Farthing 2010, 183). Such an argument is located in the knowledge that the success of a stable or healthy democracy is inherently dependent on the support of the citizens, and that voting is the ultimate test of support and an expression about a democratic system. As such, the exclusion of any group from the process suggests that a problem exists with the democratic process.

In most instances, political apathy contributes to low voter participation, especially among the youth (which makes up the sample for this study). In this instance, it is not apathy, which contributes to this problem. The quote below represents a view shared by most of the interviewees and explains the problem and the solution:

> Part of the thing is yes we want to participate, but we don't want to participate through another individual. We want to be able to participate on our own...so once those facilities are in place then I think that would be a benefit (Interviewee 1).

Lack of 'convenience' is the main problem identified by the interviewees as the challenge to voter participation among this group. In the last decade, there have been many attempts to get youth, in particular, to vote during national elections through convenience voting. Convenience voting is typically understood to mean any mode of balloting other than precinct-place voting (Gronke et al. 2008, 438). There are many different forms of convenience voting. These include early in-person voting, voting-by-mail (VBM) – providing citizens the opportunity to cast ballots by mail, calling in a vote, voting by fax, absentee voting and Internet voting. 'Every convenience voting method aims to give potential voters easier access to the ballot' (Gronke et al. 2008, 438).

Lack of convenience has been recognized throughout the literature as a contributing factor to low voter participation (Aldrich 1993; Anne-Marie Oostveen and van den Besselaar 2004a; Dyck and Gimpel 2005; Haspel and Knotts 2005). Distance/location, age, disability, and laziness often discourage citizens from accessing the voting station. Making the process of voting more convenient, it is argued, can address this problem and help to strengthen democracy (Carter and Bélanger 2012; Anne-Marie Oostveen and van den Besselaar 2004b). According to P. Gronke et al., '[a]number of studies, relying on different time periods and different sets of cases, find that convenience voting has a positive effect on turnout' (2008, 442).

Empirical evidence regarding the impact of convenience voting on voter turnout is still emerging (Kousser and Mullin 2007). However, the dominant view among researchers suggests that 'convenience voting has a small but statistically significant impact on turnout' (Gronke et al. 2008, 442; See also Magleby 1987; Karp and Banducci 2000; Southwell and Burchett 2000; Peters 2003). More recent discussions about the contributive value of convenience voting have drawn attention to the use of information and communication technologies (ICTs) specifically the Internet as a tool to strengthen democracy. This is referred to as the electronic democracy or e-democracy (Olphert and Damodaran 2007; Coleman and Blumler 2009; T. B. Riley 2003; Palvia and Sharma 2007).

Though there are many other alternatives, ICTs were also identified by the interviewees as solutions that would encourage voting among visually impaired persons. All the interviewees were of the belief that once blind persons were given more autonomy, they would participate more. ICTs would increase their level of autonomy and 'empower them'. There was a consensus among those interviewed that ICTs would make more visually impaired people want to vote because it was believed that these technologies would guarantee their independence and privacy. There was also a general view that the government should investigate a form of technology which could facilitate disabled persons. The interviewees identified various ICT related solutions to protect visually impaired persons during the voting process in other countries around the world and were desirous of these technologies being used in Caribbean countries.

Equitable Access to Government Services

Access to government services online was another theme that emerged from the data analysed. According to the World Bank, '[i]ncreasing transition of government services, records, and paperwork to digital formats can assist visually impaired citizens to access much needed information to ensure their civic and social inclusion' (Raja 2016, 16). In the last decade, several countries around the world have extended government services to the online world with the aim of enhancing efficiency and effectiveness of the delivery of public services by governments. In both countries, more so in Jamaica, there has also been an attempt to provide government services online. This is referred to as electronic government or e-government. E-government, it is argued, has wide implications for promoting good governance, democracy, and development especially among developing countries (Mofleh, Wanous, and Strachan 2008; Center for Democracy and Technology and the Information for Development Program 2002).

It has been well established in theory and practice that an effective and efficient government contributes to good governance and, by extension, 'development' (Mofleh, Wanous, and Strachan 2008; Center for Democracy and Technology and the Information for Development Program 2002; Sachs 2005; Resnick and Birner 2006; Gisselquist 2012) . Efficiency, effectiveness, and public service delivery in government mean that processes, people, structures, institutions, and actors produce results that meet specific targets while making the best use of existing resources. Today, these targets include, among other things, the adoption of an enterprise approach, scaling operations, establishing monitoring and performance evaluation systems, engaging citizens, providing timely results, research and development, competition, change management systems, divestment, sharing services across agencies and organizations, reducing costs, clear reporting systems, establishing smaller teams, increasing the quality of public service and less bureaucracy (Grindle 2007).

E-government can facilitate online accessibility, internal efficiency, and transparency of government, promote sustainable business opportunities and transform the culture and structure of government towards providing better services to citizens (Lee 2010).

There are many e-government models that can be implemented in order to achieve such outcomes. Some of these include: the use of software applications to monitor and evaluate performance; the sharing of information electronically across and within the public sector; conducting internal and external surveys about government services; cutting the waiting time for processing various government and citizen applications; conducting financial transactions between governments and businesses; the development of web portals which allow citizens to access information, conduct transactions, be consulted, become involved and engaged government employees; as well as the use of various hardware and software applications to transform the internal operations of government agencies to enhance productivity, transparency, accountability, efficiency, and effectiveness.

Saber, Srivastava, and Hossain (2006) have observed that for the aforementioned reasons, governments all over the world have embraced the idea of e-government. Y.N. Chen et al. (2006) noted that Australia, United Kingdom, United States, and Canada are pioneers in e-government and have achieved great success in their use of ICTs. With such success stories, more countries have, over the years, been implementing e-government initiatives. In India, China, and parts of Africa, as well as Latin America, ICTs are being used to streamline government activities and connect government institutions and agents more closely with the citizens they are supposed to serve (United Nations 2014; Warkentin et al. 2002).

E-Government in Jamaica

Electronic government, at least from the supply side, is nothing new in Jamaica. For several years, the government of Jamaica has undertaken a programme to transform the public sector to create greater efficiency, effectiveness, and service delivery throughout government agencies (Jamaica Information Service 2009; The Cabinet Office 2002). Most of the activities under the modernization programme have centred on the implementation of ICTs and the attendant training for public sector employees. Some of these activities include: ICT competency training for senior management, hardware and software implementation, training to build capacity at various levels and qualified computer literate technical staff, centralizing and collaborating information across some government agencies, for example, introducing government wide area network (GovNet) to facilitate the 'harmonisation of ICT infrastructure and systems across the public sector and strengthen the capacity of public institutions to deliver efficient and effective public goods and services' (Linton 2013, 1; see also CITO 2005). The government also had to establish the legal and regulatory frameworks for an effective e-government environment in Jamaica. An early example was the 2007 Electronic Transaction Act, designed to facilitate electronic transactions and connected matters. The 2010 Cybercrimes Act, criminal sanction for the misuse of data or computer systems and the abuse of electronic means of completing transactions and the 2011 Interception of Communication Act which provides for the interception of communications sent by means of telecommunications networks as well as for connected matters were subsequently enacted (Ministry of Justice 2015).

E-Government in Barbados

According to the United Nations 2016 e-Government Survey, the 'strategic framework for e-government implementation was established by the Barbados Government in 2006 and has since continuously adjusted its strategy to cope with the emerging challenges in service delivery' (United Nations Department of Economic and Social Affairs 2016, 60–61). The Barbados Ministry of Civil Service has chronicled the development of e-government in Barbados, noting that e-governance has matured in Barbados by the government's implementation of several policies, programmes, and projects aimed at increasing both the e-government sector to be better able to provide service to the Barbadian people as well as to increase the public's perception and appreciation of ICTs.

As a first step, the government of Barbados drafted and passed its *E-Government Strategy* to provide a guiding framework for e-government initiatives across the country in all sectors. Not many countries that are pursuing e-government development have e-government strategies or have strategies that are discernibly effective as in Barbados.

Secondly, the government of Barbados has instituted an *institutional framework for e-government*. The aim of this framework is to establish structure and uniformity in managing the e-government sector. The establishment and implementation of this framework increases the proficiency and the legitimacy of the sector by ensuring standards and guidelines are in place to ensure the best functionality of the sector.

Thirdly, the government of Barbados has established a *government wide area network* which provides the government with an avenue to rationalize its data and voice network to increase the government's capacity as well as to make it more responsive. According to the Barbados Ministry of Civil Service (2013), a government wide area network has created the following advantages:

- Reduced operational cost through standardization, consolidation of hardware and human resources and economies of scale;
- The ability to leverage the buying power thus reducing the costs of acquiring broadband/Internet access.

- High-speed inter-agency connections for greater communication and service delivery efficiencies;
- Extensive utilization of IP telephony with resultant cost savings;
- Provision of new secure modes of communication between government and citizens;
- Easier sharing and dissemination of information between all stakeholders;
- Facilitated deployment of enterprise-wide applications and services which enable improved and re-engineered government operations such as budgeting, financial management, human resource management, payroll and procurement, records management; and
- The ability to meet pent-up demand for connectivity across government and within ministries and agencies.

All of these benefits provided by a government wide area network are evidence of the ways in which ICTs advanced the proficiency of government through e-government. Another key development of e-government in Barbados is the *establishment of an e-government interoperability framework*. Interoperability has been a key issue in e-governance across the world with many countries that have been unable to achieve this. A lack of interoperability has rendered many state-of-the-art e-government policies inefficient simply because they do not allow government agencies to share information and use software and data formats across multiple government agencies. Interoperability helps to increase the central government's ability to police other government agencies and bodies to increase accountability, transparency, and good governance.

In addition, the government of Barbados enjoys the benefit of an *electronic document and record management system* which it refers to as *e-cabinet*. This places the collection, storage, processing, distribution, and retrieval of data at the fingertips. The system eliminates government processing times and reduces citizens' waiting time for government issued documents. This is clear efficiency of government when government agencies can manage data at high speeds to increase its capacity to provide service to citizens. This is also factored into the government's interoperability framework to increase the sharing of the data from this system among government agencies to even limit and reduce citizens' travel from one government agency to the next trying to process a single statutory requirement. These steps have demonstrated Barbados' advancement in e-government thereby making it the highest-ranking Caribbean island in relation to ICT and e-government in the Caribbean.

Based on the 2016 United Nations e-Government Survey, Barbados is well advanced as it relates to e-government. As a matter of fact, Barbados is ranked high on the e-Government Development Index (EGDI), between 0.50 and 0.75 whereas Jamaica is ranked as in the middle of the EDGI, between 0.25 and 0.50.

Barbados is recognized for its e-government especially how it has incorporated e-democracy whereby citizens are able to log on to a given website and access information on government legislations and policies and general happenings, as well as to make suggestions to government on how to improve areas of the government to be more responsive to citizens. Moreover, the government has its own website giving citizens access to government public records and enabling them to keep abreast of government activities. The government of Barbados has even gone digital with many of its government functions now having, for example, digital payroll management systems, electronic property rights registration, electronic tax declaration processes, electronic social welfare application processes, and even digital land registry management processes.

E-Government and the Visually Impaired: The Caribbean Experience

Despite these advancements, many of the interviewees argued that the e-government services that existed were not user friendly specifically for visually impaired individuals. There was a belief among all those persons interviewed that the visually impaired are generally never regarded in the architecture and accessibility of this website. And therefore, it was difficult to navigate government websites particularly those that provided government services online. In the words of one interviewee, 'the government does not make their website accessible to persons with visual disabilities, as they don't have the necessary tools to enable a screen reading software to have full access to these websites' (Interviewee 3). In this instance, the screen reading software was not speaking to the software/format used to convert the documents online.

The concern here is about Web accessibility or making the Web contents available for the persons regardless of their surrounding environment or their disability (Abu-Doush et al. 2013 See also; Mankoff, Fait, and Tran 2005; Kumar and Best 2006; Craven and Nietzio 2007). Some Web accessibility features include:

- Large text size to enhance the visibility of the fonts
- Providing descriptive links to enable users to select the most appropriate link

- Use of contrasted colours (i.e. between background and text) to improve the visibility of the contents (Abu-Doush et al. 2013, 275).

The literature on Web accessibility suggests that making Web contents available for the persons regardless of their surrounding environment or their disability is a global challenge (Jaeger 2006; Kuzma 2009; Shi 2006; Rabaiah and Vandijck 2009). Certainly, for the visually impaired and those interested in this area of research, policy, and work, this is problematic and should not be the norm as stated by I. Abu-Doush et al. (2013). There are two critical factors: the first is that the:

> ...United Nations Convention on the Rights of Disabled Persons established a commitment from the governments to give people with disabilities equal rights to access different facilities provided to the society (United Nations Enable 2010). It also stated that measures should be taken to guarantee the accessibility of technologies and the accessibility of physical environment (273).

The second being:

> The World Wide Web Consortium (W3C) is an organisation for standardisation of the Web. It provides a set of accessibility recommendations called Web Contents Accessibility Guidelines (WCAG 2.0). These guidelines entail a set of recommendations for Web developers to provide a Web contents which are universally accessible (i.e. can be accessed by people with different kinds of disabilities). Another set of rules are introduced in Section 508 (2010), which require that the electronic information for the US government must be accessible to people with disabilities (Ibid.).

Indeed, these international conventions and protocol as well as government must hold software and hardware developers and companies accountable to these standards if we are to take them seriously and encourage and promote the kind of inclusiveness and equity we aspire to create for PWDs.

Inclusion in the Decision-Making Process of Government

Consultations with all the citizens of a society and including them in the decision-making process is a key ingredient of democracy today. All citizens should be able to follow and understand the decision-making process (transparency) and must feel that their interests are taken into consideration (inclusion and equity). Many of the interviewees from both Jamaica and Barbados believed that they were wholly excluded from the decision-making process that allows the visually impaired to envision democracy.

They argue that when governments embark on any new policies, particularly those that will affect persons with disability, they are not fully engaged in the process. The interviewees believed that the disabled should be consulted as a group in the same way other groups such as the private sector and other civil society groups are consulted and more so, taken seriously. 'This puts us at a great disadvantage' said Interviewee 2. According to him, 'people are making decisions for us and about us, who don't know anything about us, who have not lived our lives' (Interviewee 2). Many of the interviewees argue that the disabled community should be engaged about these policies more. Accordingly:

...we should be consulted as how they consult the other groups such as the private sector and also other civil society groups because they need to know our input within policies to ensure that any policies that is formulated and implemented is not to work against us; doesn't lead to us having a disadvantage (Interviewee 1).

Another challenge identified by the participants was the type of information that they had access to. Some of the interviewees contend, 'although we had some information, current affairs, international information, information from newspapers, information in the media and so on, we do not have access to everything' (Interviewee 10). The interviewee further lamented:

The media and government information services are selective in what information they put out. Sometimes we don't get the whole picture. We don't have all the information and therefore we are not able to understand or know exactly what is going on all the time". We have to make decisions based on what we get access to and when we go in search of the information there are many roadblocks. For example, legislation for parliamentary documents are not always gazetted and that when they are gazetted they are not put an audio files or they are not in digital format. This is always the case with old policy documents which will have the historical information. Information that we will need in order to make informed choices (Interviewee 10).

According to the interviewees, governments should ensure that all official documents are digitized and that all the national libraries have audio storage facilities with these documents. There was also a view that governments should enhance the quality of the website from just image, so that a blind person could use their JAWS to read the legislation and other items. According to one interviewee speaking about the government information website in Jamaica:

...most things stand, most of the things you see on the JIS website and the GOJ website, you notice that those are scanned documents. Therefore, it's not compatible for the JAWS to read those (Interviewee 1).

This, many of the interviewees argued, would encourage greater participation among visually impaired persons, in the democratic framework.

Some Solutions

It was clear from the interviews that most of the respondents believed that the appropriate ICTs can be used to adequately engage visually impaired citizens and engender or empower them to actively participate in the democratic space beyond simple knowledge, awareness, and political talk between and among other citizens. 'Appropriate ICTs' are the integrated and participatory approachs that result in tools and processes for establishing information and communication technologies (ICT) that are suitable for the cultural, environmental, organizational, economic, and political conditions in which it is intended to be used (van Reijswoud 2009, 6). In other words, technologies that meet the needs of *all* of the users.

In this context, appropriate ICTs are those ICTs that are suitable for the circumstances of visually impaired people – technologies that meet the needs of visually impaired individuals. Generally speaking, ICTs are also seen as a good solution for the challenges that visually impaired persons have in substantive participation in the Jamaican political landscape. Indeed, there is a general recognition among the interviewees that the government of Jamaica is doing extensive work to make ICTs accessible in Jamaica. According to one interviewee, 'we have more people utilizing social media to express their opinions on politics, whether it's by Twitter or Facebook' (Interviewee 1). He further stated:

> With ICTs now, I mean, information you don't necessarily have to go into a library and search for this extended period to find information; you don't necessarily have to... you have more options in terms of media and also persons who are blind, we never had access to the print media. But what the ICT has enabled us to do is read what is happening within the newspapers via the JAWS- which is a speech reading software (Interviewee 1).

Jamaica, for example, is regarded as being advanced in the use and application of ICTs and also in relation to access to ICTs. The Jamaican ICT sector is among the best in the world (Angus 2013). Since the emergence of the ICT for development debate, successive governments have implemented several legal, regulatory, and policy frameworks to establish, improve, and sustain the Jamaican ICT industry. These have included the Data Protection Act, Amendment of Cybercrime Act, establishment of cybersecurity policy/framework, and a cyber emergency response team to name a few. Additionally, since 2013, successive governments have rolled out the island-wide broadband network and the establishment of community access points to engage citizens better and to increase and improve utility of ICT platforms. On the same note and more recently, the government has commenced the establishment of rules, and the implementation of the number portability system that will allow greater interoperability between and among telecommunication networks in the country. These levels of advanced ICTs are expected to stimulate growth in the economy by creating more informed citizens, resulting in increased social and technical competencies in this globally competitive community.

On the note of building and increasing competencies of the people in respect to ICTs, successive governments have embarked on a mission to comprehensively complete the high-school phase of its E-learning Jamaica programme to ensure that young people across the island are being sufficiently exposed to and are in receipt of the tremendous benefits of ICTs in education. The Central Information Technology Office (CITO), which was established in 2001 as the enabler for national development through its charge to formulate, update, coordinate, and monitor implementation of the National Information and Communications Technology Strategy, has been incorporated into the Ministry of Energy, Science and Technology. The Ministry has been charged with the responsibility for ICT-related activities in an effort to streamline ICT management in the country as well as to achieve greater uniformity of the ICT sector in Jamaica. On the note of uniformity, the government of Jamaica is currently pursuing the implementation of a common government-wide area network which seeks to incorporate and integrate all government ministries, departments, agencies in one overall public sector communications network.

On the side of innovation, there have been spirited talks concerning the government's proposed plan to introduce mobile money. The Bank of Jamaica guidelines to drive this process have already been issued and the Development Bank of Jamaica's Mobile Money for Microfinance Pilot Project has already been launched. Feedback from different agents is being processed to assess the viability of launching it for access to wider cross sections of the society.

Since 2005, successive Jamaican governments have attempted to implement several e-governance projects most of which aim to expand access to government services for citizens.

Most recently, and as stated above, many government agencies have migrated many of their services to the Internet and in particular to online social networks such as Facebook. Currently, most government agencies have Facebook pages, which allow for interaction between citizens and government. In addition to this, political parties and aspiring politicians are also using social media to connect with citizens. This practice was influenced by Barack Obama's use of social media during the 2008 US Presidential Elections. Since then, there has been an increasing use of social media for political campaigning in Jamaica. The two major political parties – the People's National Party and the Jamaica Labour Party – have both intensified their social media presence. Indeed, during the last general election in 2016, both parties launched substantive social media e-campaigns to utilize ICT to garner support in the election period.

Since February 2016, the Jamaican government has made a concerted effort to use ICTs to foster the economic development of the country. Most recently, the government outlined its ten-point plan for the development of the information and communication technology (ICT) sector and Jamaica's transformation into a 'truly digital society facilitate significant investments, generate economic growth, and create jobs for the people of Jamaica'. According to the Minister of Science, Energy and Technology, Dr Andrew Wheatley, the government

> ...considers the ICT sector one of the main drivers of economic growth, and we recognise how important it is to place greater attention on extracting the direct and indirect economic benefits that may be derived from a focused ICT strategy.

Under the ten-point plan, the government said it would:
- Establish true universal access by providing free Internet access to essential Government and educational services for every citizen.
- Introduce eHOME (the electronic home-office mode of employment). This 'work from home' initiative will, among other things, boost productivity, empower workers, and generate cost savings to both employees and the government.
- Make Jamaica the Caribbean's leading producer of technology, not just consumers of technology, by creating a technology innovation fund to provide sustainable financing of technology-based projects and start-ups.
- Work closely with the Ministry of Education to ensure holistic, efficient and effective use of technology to support teaching and

learning as well as improved education administration throughout the system.

- Collaborate closely with the new Ministry of Economic Growth and Job Creation to broaden support for business process outsourcing beyond just call-centre services so employment opportunities for university graduates and professionals are expanded.

- Drive better ICT governance practices throughout government to make it more efficient and make information more accessible, including use of the corps of young people trained through the National Service Programme and National Apprenticeship Programme.

- Repeal the 15-year-old Telecommunications Act and replace it with a new ICT Act. Harmonise all relevant ICT legislation to ensure cohesion across the regulatory elements of ICT to create a more modern fit for purpose framework, including creation of a single ICT regulator.

- Promulgate and pass into law: Data Protection, Data Privacy & Sharing Acts.

- Drive the review, repeal and update of the Electronic Transactions Act with its subsequent reassignment to the technology portfolio.

- Introduce comprehensive e-Waste Management policy and legislation to establish protocols for the recycling, rehabilitation, reuse and proper disposal of such electronic waste as laptop and desktop computers, tablets, cellular telephones, television sets, radios, air conditioning units, refrigerators, batteries, and other household appliances (*Jamaica Observer* 2016).

These are unquestionably important developments, but how does the introduction of these ICTs influence the lives of visually impaired citizens? Many of the visually impaired Jamaicans who were interviewed see the advances in ICTs as beneficial to them in their social and political lives. They also recognized, as stated above, that much more is needed to facilitate their full inclusion and engender an equitable playing field.

For many of the persons interviewed, appropriate ICTs also means inexpensive ICTs. Many of the visually impaired in Jamaica and Barbados require substantive financial assistance to access many of the technologies needed for them to be fully included in the decision-making process of their countries. As in many instances, these technologies may be inaccessible because of the cost associated with them. Indeed, being able to afford ICTs was a major concern of several of the interviewees. This raises the question of the digital divide.

The digital divide is a term used to refer to a state of unequal access to digital technology within or between countries. It is the gap between those who have access to ICTs/ICT infrastructure as well as the availability of ICTs/ICT infrastructure, and those who do not. The digital divide is also a function of awareness, knowledge, information, education and capacity. In other words, the capability of citizens to actually use or afford these technologies even when they are available (Lau 2003; Belanger and Carter 2006). The digital divide has excluded many citizens in the developing world from engaging in e-government related activities, and in so doing, the divide undermines the democratic processes in these countries. Taken to its extreme, the digital divide threatens good governance and development.

Though Jamaicans and Barbadians have accepted using different types of ICTs in their everyday life, like the citizens of Trinidad and Tobago (Bissessar 2010), not many Jamaicans or Barbadians can actually use these ICTs to access e-government services. Jamaica has a population of 2.8 million people, of which 38.7 per cent have access to the Internet (Internet Society 2014). Computers are expensive relative to average wages, and the Internet is also out of reach of most Jamaicans. One-third of the population, those who are living below the poverty line, cannot access an Internet connection, for one reason or another. Indeed, many of the individuals in this sector can barely afford their basic needs. Internet access is not a priority and may not even be in their contemplation.

This, of course, means that many of the e-government initiatives aimed at enhancing the efficiency and effectiveness of government as well as public service delivery are not having the wide-reaching impact that might be expected. The government of Jamaica is currently attempting to address this divide by installing computer access points across the country. In addition, there are several other initiatives geared to promoting easier access to the Internet in Jamaica. One example is the 'International Students Tablet Programme' which was initiated in 2012. Through this programme computer tablets were distributed to inner-city youths for educational purposes. Another example of an initiative was the provision of free Internet access throughout public libraries across Jamaica in 2007.

The visually impaired are particularly challenged by this divide. Certainly, many of the persons interviewed for this study spoke of having financial challenges, mostly resulting from an inability to find substantive employment because of their 'condition'. These challenges make it problematic to procure the ICT needed to adequately meet their specific needs. The challenge of the digital divide must be addressed if visually impaired citizens are to fully capitalize on the availability of ICTs and use them as a catalyst for inclusion. One recommendation offered by an interviewee bears considering:

> ...the government needs to form public/private partnerships with telecommunications providers to source the best technology and if they can reduce the duties and so on, on these technologies then we will have far more access to information and more persons who are disabled would be empowered to participate in the democratic process (Interviewee 1).

Several other Jamaican interviewees also mentioned the need for more government support to visually impaired citizens as it relates to the provision of access to ICTs. Beyond the lack of government support, however, some of the individuals who were interviewed also identified the lack of innovation in providing and promoting the use of ICTs by many civil society organizations that have been established to support them. This lack of innovation also contributes to the lack of inclusion and equity among the visually impaired. One interviewee suggested, for example, that the avenues through which visually impaired Jamaicans have a voice are mainly advocacy groups, which are ineffective, or as he puts it, 'are not working as effectively as we'd want them to be'. They are not as aggressive as an organization should be in terms of advocacy. They have no teeth. Consequently, many persons with disabilities are not heard. Another interviewee felt that the organizations were not innovative in the solutions that they provide.

Conclusion

Visually impaired citizens in the Caribbean may believe that they have a stake in the society, but they also believe that they are not given the opportunity to have a voice to substantively participate in the decision-making process of their country. The chapter explored the primary challenges that visually impaired Caribbean citizens face regarding the use of ICTs to access and participate in the democratic space and some possible solutions. The need for (1) equitable opportunities in the voting process, (2) equitable access to government services, as well as (3) inclusion in the decision-making process were identified as challenges faced by visually impaired Caribbean citizens. There is a need for ICT related solutions to address these challenges to empower visually impaired citizens to be fully integrated in the democratic space.

Chapter 7
Conclusion:
Assistive Democracy

Introduction

This qualitative study had four objectives. The first was to understand how and in what ways ICTs have aided visually impaired Caribbean citizens to access and participate in the democratic space. It was observed that ICTs have contributed substantively to the lives of many (but certainly not all) visually impaired in improving their political knowledge and promoting political talk. It was also highlighted that ICTs did not engender the type of inclusion and equity that they were desirous of. The second objective was to determine the extent to which ICTs have addressed the challenges of equity and inclusion faced by visually impaired Caribbean citizens. The findings revealed that though ICTs did encourage political talk and knowledge, this still did not translate into substantive 'inclusion' nor 'equity' among the visually impaired participants at least where accessing the democratic space was concerned.

The third objective was to identify primary challenges that visually impaired Caribbean citizens experience in using ICTs to access and participate in the democratic space. Three themes emerged from the data analysed. The first was equity in the voting process: independent and private participation; the second was equitable access to government services; and the third was inclusion in the decision-making process of government. The fourth and final objective was to highlight and place necessary emphasis on the solutions offered by visually impaired citizens in terms of mitigating the challenges faced using ICTs to access and participate in the democratic space, based on their own experiences. These solutions would be based on the voices of visually impaired citizens. Visually impaired participants believe that governments should, through investigation, provide them with more appropriate ICTs; technologies that meet their specific needs. The primary themes that emerged from this study suggest that appropriate ICTs are tools that can empower visually impaired citizens and enable them to engage the democratic space independently. Emerging innovations in ICTs that enable visually impaired individuals to participate in the democratic space are discussed in the next section.

E-Democracy: The Future

The potential of e-democracy to facilitate political talk, promote political knowledge, empower citizens with disabilities to engage online government services and actors and allow active participation in the democratic process with regard to voting, referenda, petitions, campaigning, community building/collaborative environments, debates, consultations and meetings is undeniable. New developments in ICTs look very promising for persons with disabilities, especially those citizens with visual challenges. Many computer and software development companies are designing applications to assist persons with disabilities including visually impaired citizens which can be used to facilitate inclusion and equity in the democratic space. The development of new interactive devices such as touch, gesture, and speech will make it easier for visually impaired individuals, in particular, to be able to access data by speaking to the computer. Indeed, there are many appropriate ICTs around to facilitate e-democracy specifically and assist democracy generally. Several companies have been developing solutions for persons with disabilities.

Autonomous Cars

The need for independence and privacy were two major challenges identified by the persons interviewed for this study, but so was a lack of mobility. A lack of mobility prevents the visually impaired from going to polling stations, attending political meetings, visiting Parliament and the offices of their representatives, to name a few. Autonomous cars can solve this challenge. Autonomous cars are vehicles that are capable of sensing their environment and navigating without human input. Autonomous motor vehicles are based on a combination of laser, radar, and 3D environment data and GPS. Autonomous motor vehicles essentially drive on their own. Sometimes referred to as a driverless car, self-driving car, or robotic cars, Autonomous motor vehicles use radar, lidar, GPS, odometry, and computer vision to navigate across or throughout cities. Examples of these cars include the Google self-driving car developed by Google X.

In 2012, Steve Mahan, a visually impaired citizen of San Francisco, USA became one of the first persons to drive in a Google self-driving car. In the YouTube video posted by Google, Mahan walks out of his house and steps into his car. Once seated, the car's engine comes on and when the car leaves his carport it announces, 'auto driving'. The car exits Mahan's neighbourhood and Mahan takes the vehicle for a drive through the local drive-through restaurant and later collects his dry cleaning without any difficulty. In a news report on ABC news 7, Mahan said, 'It's like riding with a fabulous driver.' Mahan continued, 'Anybody who spends five minutes out in that traffic will realize that the danger are the humans. Personally, I can't wait for the robots to start driving' (ABC News 7, 1). According to Mahan, 'I'm finding there's a lot of buzz, a lot of people in the blind community talking about driverless cars' (Rose 2013). He felt that autonomous cars would give him the flexibility and independence to do the things he wants to do and go the places he wants to go. This could easily mean going to the polling station, a political rally, to parliament, to meet with a political representative or join a political protest.

Four states in the United States – California, Michigan, Florida and Nevada – have passed legislation to make autonomous cars legal. It is expected that others will follow and many believe this will pave the way for a global revolution in the use of autonomous cars. Already, major car companies such as Audi, Mercedes-Benz, BMW, Toyota, Nissan, Bocsh and Tesla have experimented and continue to experiment with several features of autonomous motor vehicles. These cars could be used in controlled environments like highways by 2020. Thus, in the near future, scenes from feature films such as *Minority Report* (2002), *I, Robot* (2004), The *Fifth Element* (1997) and *Total Recall* (1990) which depicted the widespread use of autonomous cars could well become a fact not fiction.

Voting Solutions

Getting to the polling station is just one part of voter participation for visually impaired citizens. Voting is the critical part. There are many solutions available to visually impaired citizens which can allow them independence and privacy. Hart InterCivic is one solution. Hart InterCivic is a full-service election solutions innovator which provides secure, accurate and reliable voting solutions which include: ballots with Braille labels; audio ballots accessible through headphones; audible sounds to alert voters who are blind or visually impaired if their ballot contains mismarks that require attention; instructions in Braille and large print and easy mobility for curb side voting were allowed. Hart InterCivic voting solutions for the visually impaired is recognized as an innovative way of facilitating inclusion and equity for this group of citizens.

Other more advanced ICT-type solutions include iVotronic from Election Systems & Software, the AVC Edge from Sequoia Voting Systems, the eSlate from Hart InterCivic, and the Vote-Trakker from Avante International Technology. These solutions allow visually impaired citizens to vote in private and verifiably and so eliminate the need for an assistant. All machines allow visually impaired citizens to review their ballot via a speech output using headphones. A touch screen technology allows them to scroll through the ballot and choose their candidates. Figure 7.1 provides a more detailed description of each solution:

Figure 7.1: Innovative ICT Voting Solutions

iVotronic

The iVotronic touch-screen voting unit is incorporated into a private, sturdy, portable voting booth that could fold up and be rolled on its wheels. The voting unit can be removed and placed on the lap of a voter using a wheelchair or taken out to the street in areas that allow curbside voting. The touch-screen display measures 9.75 inches by 7.25 inches, and the unit has four buttons that blind voters use to navigate and mark the ballot. Three of these buttons are on the panel in front of the touch screen, including two yellow Up and Down triangular buttons. To the right of these two buttons is a green diamond-shaped Select button. In the middle of the panel in back of the touch screen is a black oval Vote button. A red light in this button flashes when it is time to cast the final ballot.

AVC Edge

The AVC Edge is another touch-screen unit. The voting unit is consolidated into its own portable voting booth, but the booth is not as sturdy as the iVotronic booth and does not offer quite as much privacy in its design. Although the touch screen does not detach for curbside voting, the booth does have a wide stance for wheelchair access. The touch-screen display measures 9 inches by 12 inches, and can be adjusted to an angle that is more easily reached for seated voters. Voters who are blind use a handheld control box featuring four tactilely identifiable buttons labelled in Braille. The top right button is a square blue Help button, the bottom right button is a red round Select button, and on the left are two triangular buttons pointing Up and Down. The top button is green and is labelled Next, and the bottom one is yellow and is labelled Back.

eSlate

The eSlate voting machine is not a touch-screen unit, so both sighted and blind voters use the same push-button interface. Although it is available with its own voting booth, our test unit did not come with a booth. The unit is portable to accommodate curbside voting. It includes a headphone jack to provide privacy to voters who are blind or visually impaired. In addition, the unit can be controlled by two tactile switches that voters can operate using their elbows or feet, if need be. It also has a port to connect a 'sip and puff' device that a person with quadriplegia can use to control the voting unit with his or her mouth.

Vote-Trakker

The Vote-Trakker is a portable touch-screen unit with speech output generated via synthetic speech, rather than human voice recordings. The unit did not come with a voting booth, but it did have a glare guard that folds out over the screen to provide some privacy. The touch screen is 11 inches wide by 8.5 inches high. The interface used by voters who are blind or visually impaired is a modified QWERTY computer keyboard. The Escape, Minus, Enter, and Control keys on the four corners of the keyboard are the primary controls, and these keys are raised about twice as high as the other keys for easy identification. In addition, the arrow keys can be used for scrolling, and the letter keys are used to write in candidates.

Source: AFB AccessWorld Magazine, http://www.afb.org/afbpress/pub.asp?docid=aw030603

Assistive Democracy: Towards a Categorization of Visually Impaired Solutions for the Democratic Space

Certainly, much of the discussions surrounding assistive technology normally focuses on the use of technologies to enable PWDs particularly as it relates to social and economic well-being. The literature surrounding democratic well-being is scarce. Indeed, a new paradigm is needed to focus on creating an enabling environment for PWDs to be included in the democratic space, to encourage their participation, and to foster equity in this space. Generally speaking, a paradigm which narrows or reduces thinking and innovations towards the use of ICTs to promote, engender, encourage e-democracy for PWDs ultimately enables them to envision democracy.

'Democracy' is perhaps one of the most used terms in the world today and yet it is also one of the most value-laden, controversial, and problematic terms in existence. It has evolved since its appearance in ancient Greek philosophical and political thought and it is still evolving. There are many definitions of democracy some more substantive than others (Becker 1958; Rodrik and Wacziarg 2005). The most recognized definition of democracy is of 'a government in which the supreme power is vested in the people and exercised by them directly or indirectly through a system of representation usually involving periodically held free elections'. The simplest definition which is of significance to this work is the one that says that democracy is a type of political system where all members in the democracy have equal share of power. In other words, 'rule by the people.' Among other things is the guaranteed equity and inclusion for all citizens. Democracy as a process has also evolved over the years. Democracy has veered in multiple directions representing many different forms, types, systems, and processes. This in part is what contributes to the multiplicity of definitions and problems with application. Assistive technology emerges as a typology, which is endemic of the disabled community and can be used as a part of any discourse articulating types of technologies which aid persons with disabilities to access the democratic space.

Assistive democracy draws motivation from the principle of assistive technologies (Vanderheiden 1998; Hersh and Johnson 2010; Scherer and Glueckauf 2005; Cook and Polgar 2015). Assistive technologies are tools that enable and/or improve the lives and livelihoods of persons with disabilities. These tools include wheelchairs, keyboards that are larger- or smaller-than-standard keys or keyboards, electronic pointing devices, wands, and sticks that can be worn on the head, held in the mouth or strapped to the chin, which are used to press keys on the keyboard, joysticks, trackballs, and touch screens. Assistive technologies also include Braille embossers, on-screen keyboards, refreshable Braille displays, screen enlargers, or screen magnifiers and software applications such as screen readers, speech recognition or voice recognition programmes, text-to-speech (TTS) or speech synthesizers as well as talking and large-print word processors.

Assistive democracy explains and describes the general use of technologies to specifically assist and enable people with disabilities to successfully access all aspects of the democratic space through the use of tools and techniques. Assistive democracy facilitates the political processes enabling persons with disabilities such as visually impaired citizens to vote independently, vote within private settings; empowering these same citizens with the capabilities for political talk and capacities to access information to enhance their political knowledge. Assistive democracy also encourages and enables citizens with disabilities to engage online government services and actors and allows them to actively participate in the democratic process with regard to voting, referendums, petitions, campaigning, community building/collaborative environments, debates, consultations, meetings and so on. Assistive democracy thus facilitates all other forms, types and systems of democracy. E-democracy can therefore be seen as a type of assistive democracy. So too are any tools which engender the type of desired outcomes of persons with disabilities regarding the democratic space.

Given the current and future trends in ICTs and the possibilities that ICTs may offer as tools to enable and empower people with disabilities, there is an urgent need to explore disability studies within the context of ICT being used as a main tool for democracy within its own space. Assistive democracy offers that space.

References

Abramson, M. A., and T. L. Morin. 2003. *E-Government 2003*. Rowman & Littlefield.

Abu-Doush, I., A. Bany-Mohammed, E. Ali, and M. A. Al-Betar. 2013. Towards a More Accessible E-Government in Jordan: An Evaluation Study of Visually Impaired Users and Web Developers. *Behaviour & Information Technology* 32, no. 3: 273–93.

ADA. 2013. What Is the Definition of Disability under the ADA? *ADA National Network*. https://adata.org/faq/what-definition-disability-under-ada.

Aldrich, J. H. 1993. Rational Choice and Turnout. *American Journal of Political Science* 37, no. 1: 246–78.

Allsopp, D. H., K. Colucci, E. Doone, L. Perez, E. Bryant Jr., and T. N. Holhfeld. 2012. Interactive Whiteboard Technology for Students with Disabilities: A Year-Long Exploratory Study. *Journal of Special Education Technology* 27, no. 4: 1–15.

Alvarez, R. M., L. Rae. Atkeson, and T. E. Hall. 2007. The New Mexico Election Adminstration Report: The 2006 November General Election. https://www.brennancenter.org/sites/default/.../coabc827ae56751263_y6m6b9gqy.pd.

Alvarez, R. M., and T. E. Hall. 2003. *Point, Click, and Vote: The Future of Internet Voting*. Brookings Institution Press.

Amnesty International. 2006. Sexual Violence against Women and Girls in Jamaica: 'Just a Little Sex.' *Amnesty International*. http://www.unhcr.org/refworld/docid/44c5f2a24.html.

Andersen, R., A. Heath, and R. Sinnot. 2001. Political Knowledge and Electoral Choices. 87. CREST Working Paper. Oxford. http://www.crest.ox.ac.uk/papers/p87.pdf.

———. 2002. Do Less Informed Voters Make Mistakes? Political Knowledge and Electoral Choice.97. CREST Working Paper. Oxford. http://www.crest.ox.ac.uk/papers/p97.pdf.

Anduiza, E., A. Gallego, and L. Jorba. 2012. Internet Use and the Political Knowledge Gap in Spain. *Revista Internacional de Sociología* 70, no. 1: 129–51.

Angus, Garfield L. 2013. Jamaica Has World Class ICT Industry – State Minister Robinson. *JIS Services*. http://jis.gov.jm/jamaica-has-world-class-ict-industry-state-minister-robinson/.

Asen, Robert. 2004. A Discourse Theory of Citizenship. *Quarterly Journal of Speech* 90, no. 2: 189–211.

As-Saber, S., A. Srivastava, and K. Hossain. 2006. Information Technology Law and E-Government: A Developing Country Perspective. *Journal of Administration and Governance* 1, no. 2: 84–101.

Auyero, J. 2000. The Logic of Clientelism in Argentina: An Ethnographic Account. *American Research Review* 35, no. 3: 55–81.

Aziz, Maslina Abdul, Wan Abdul Rahim Wan Mohd Isa, and Nurul Syahiralh Mohd Fadzir. 2011. Accessibility of Websites for People with Disabilities (PWD) in Malaysia: An Empirical Investigation. *International Journal on Advanced Science, Engineering and Information Technology* 1, no. 2: 221–26.

Barbados Government Information Service. 2007. Committed to Disabled Persons. http://www.barbados.gov.bb/site_search.asp?id=20079265675.txt.

Barbados Ministry of Civil Service. 2013. Barbados E-Government Programme Status Update. http://redgealc.org/download.php?len=es&id=5610&nbre=e govBARB.pdf&ti=application/pdf&tc=Contenidos.

Barber, Benjamin R. 1984. *Strong Democracy: Participatory Politics for a New Age*. Los Angeles: University of California Press.

Baxter, Graeme, and Rita Marcella. 2013. Online Parliamentary Election Campaigns in Scotland: A Decade of Research. *JeDEM* 5, no. 2: 107–27.

Becker, Gary S. 1958. Competition and Democracy. *The Journal of Law & Economics* 1: 105–9.

Becker, S. A. 2004. A Study of Web Usability for Older Adults Seeking Online Health Resources. *ACM Transactions on Computer-Human Interaction (TOCHI)*. http://dl.acm.org/citation.cfm?id=1035578.

Beddie, Lesley, Ann Macintosh, and Anna Malina. 2001. E-Democracy and the Scottish Parliament. In *Towards the E-Society: E-Commerce, E-Business, and E-Government*, edited by Beat Schmid, Katarina Stanoevska-Slabeva, and Volker Tschammer, 695–705. London: Kluwer Academic Publishers.

Belanger, F., and L. Carter. 2006. The Effects of the Digital Divide on E-Government: An Empirical Evaluation. In *Proceedings of the 39th Annual Hawaii International Conference System Sciences, 2006 HICSS 06*. Vol. 4. Hawaii.

Bennett, W. Lance. 2008. *Civic Life Online: Learning How Digital Media Can Engage Youth*. Cambridge, MA: The MIT Press.

Bissessar, A. 2010. The Challenges of E-Governance in a Small, Developing Society: The Case of Trinidad and Tobago. In *Comparative E-Government*, edited by C. G. Reddick, 313–29. New York: Springer.

Bohman, J., and W. Rehg. 1997. *Deliberative Democracy: Essays on Reason and Politics*. Cambridge, MA: MIT Press.

Bricout, J. C., and P. M. A. Baker. 2012. Deploying Information and Communication Technologies (ICT) to Enhance Participation in Local Governance for Citizens with Disabilities. In *ICTs for Advancing Rural Communities and Human Development: Addressing the Digital Divide*, edited by Susheel Chhabra. Hershey, PA: IGI Global.

Brittan, Y. 1982. The Household Income Distribution of Disabled People in the UK. *International Journal of Social Economics* 9, no. 6 and 7: 125–38.

Caldow, Janet. 2004. *E-Democracy: Putting Down Global Roots*. Institute for Electronic Government, IBM.

Carter, L., and F. Bélanger. 2012. Internet Voting and Political Participation: An Empirical Comparison of Technological and Political Factors. *ACM SIGMIS Database* 43, no. 3: 26–46.

Cato, Eddie. 2011. State of Education in Jamaica – Part 1. *Jamaica Gleaner*. jamaica-gleaner.com/gleaner/20110124/news/news2.html.

Center for Democracy and Technology and the Information for Development Program. 2002. *The E-Government Handbook for Developing Countries*. Washington, DC: World Bank.

Chen, Y.N., H.M. Chen, W. Huang, and R.K.H. Ching. 2006. E-Government Strategies in Developed and Developing Countries: An Implementation Framework and Case Study. *Journal of Global Information Management* 14, no. 1: 23–46.

Chisholm, W., G. Vanderheiden, and I. Jacobs. 2001. Web Content Accessibility Guidelines 1.0. *Interactions* 8, no. 4: 35–54.

Chrissafis, Thanassis, and Mechthild Rohen. 2010. European eParticipation Developments From Ad Hoc Experiences towards Mass Engagement. *JeDEM* 2, no. 2: 89–98.

CITO. 2005. An Effective E-Governance Framework: The Key to Enhanced E-Government Services. *Central Information Technology Office*. http://www.cito.gov.jm/files/E-Gov.

Colaizzi, Paul F. 1978. Psychological Research as the Phenomenologist Views It. In *Existential-Phenomenological Alternatives for Psychology*, edited by Ronald Valle and Mark King, 48–71. New York: Oxford University Press.

Coleman, S., and J.G. Blumler. 2009. *The Internet and Democratic Citizenship: Theory, Practice and Policy*. Cambridge: Cambridge University Press.

Colesca, S.E. 2009. Understanding Trust in E-Government. *Economics of Engineering Decisions* 3, no. 3: 7–15.

Cook, Albert M., and Janice Miller Polgar. 2015. *Assistive Technologies: Principles and Practice*. 4th ed. Mosby.

Coombs, Norman. 1990. Disability and Technology: A Historical and Social Perspective. In *Presentation for the Organization of American Historians Held in Washington DC, March, 1990*. Washington, DC: Rochester Institute of Technology.

Cowan, D., and A. Turner-Smith. 1999. The Role of Assistive Technology in Alternative Models of Care for Older People. In *With Respect to Old Age: Long Term Care – Rights and Responsibilities. Alternative Models of Care for Older People. Research Volume 2 Appendix 4*. London: The Stationery Office.

Craven, J. 2003. Access to Electronic Resources by Visually Impaired People. *Information Research* 8, no. 4: 4–8.

Craven, J., and A. Nietzio. 2007. A Task-Based Approach to Assessing the Accessibility of Web Sites. *Performance Measurement and Metrics* 8, no. 2: 98–109.

Cruickshank, Peter, Noella Edelmann, and Colin Smith. 2010. *Signing an E-Petition as a Transition from Lurking to Participation*. Trauner.

Dahl, Robert Alan. 1998. *On Democracy*. New Haven, CT: Yale University Press.

Dalton, R.J. 2004. *Democratic Challenges, Democratic Choices: The Erosion of Political Support in Advanced Industrial Democracies*. UK: Oxford University Press.

De Zúñiga, Homero Gil, Eulàlia Puig-I-Abril, and Hernando Rojas. 2009. Weblogs, Traditional Sources Online and Political Participation: An Assessment of How the Internet Is Changing the Political Environment. *New Media & Society* 11 (4): 553–74. doi:10.1177/1461444809102960.

Delli Carpini, M.X., F.L. Cook, and L.R. Jacobs. 2004. Public Deliberation, Discursive Participation, and Citizen Engagement: A Review of the Empirical Literature. *Annual Review of Political Science* 7: 315–44.

Delli Carpini, M.X., and S. Keeter. 1993. Measuring Political Knowledge: Putting First Things First. *American Journal of Political Science* 37, no. 4: 1179–1206.

———. 1996. *What Americans Know about Politics and Why It Matters*. New Haven, CT: Yale University Press.

Dodenhoff, Paul. 2015. The UK General Election 2015: What's in Store for Disability. *Disabled World*. http://www.disabled-world.com/news/uk/uk-election.php.

Done, R.S. 2003. Internet Voting: Bringing Elections to the Desktop. In *E-Government 2003*, 237–65. The PricewaterhouseCoopers Endowment for the Business of Government.

Doyal, L. 1983. Poverty and Disability in the Third World: The Crippling Effects of Underdevelopment. In *A Cry for Health. Poverty and Disability in the Third World*, edited by O Shirley. Frome.

Dube, Andrew K. 2005. The Role and Effectiveness of Disability Legislation in South Africa. http://www.addc.org.au/documents/resources/20050301-the-role-and-effectiveness-of-disability-legislation-in-south-africa_766.pdf.

Duchesne, S., and F. Haegel. 2007. Accepting or Avoiding Conflict in Public Talk. *British Journal of Political Science* 37: 1–22.

Dyck, J.J., and J.G. Gimpel. 2005. Distance, Turnout, and the Convenience of Voting. *Social Science Quarterly* 86, no. 3: 531–548.

Easton, D. 1965. *A Systems Analysis of Political Life*. New York: Wiley.

———. 1975. A Re-Assessment of the Concept of Political Support. *British Journal of Political Science* 5, no. 4: 435–57.

Ebrahim, Z., Z. Irani, and S.A. Shawi. 2003. E-Government Adoption: Analysis of Adoption Staged Models. Paper presented at 3rd European Conference on E-Government, Dublin.

Edie, Carlene J. 1989. From Manley to Seaga: The Persistence of Clientelist Politics in Jamaica. *Social and Economic Studies* 38, no. 1: 1–35.

Elder, Laurent, Heloise Emdon, Richard Fuchs, and Ben Petrazzini, eds. 2013. *Connecting ICTs to Development: The IDRC Experience*.

European Commission. 2009. Study and Supply of Services on the Development of eParticipation in the EU. http://ec.europa.eu/information_society/activities/egovernment/docs/reports/european_eparticipation_summary_nov_.

Farthing, R. 2010. The Politics of Youthful Antipolitics: Representing the 'issue' of Youth Participation in Politics. *Journal of Youth Studies* 13, no. 2: 181–95.

Fiala-Butora, J., M. A. Stein, and J. E. Lord. 2014. *The Democratic Life of the Union: Toward Equal Voting Participation for Europeans with Disabilities. Faculty Publications. Paper 1673*. William & Mary Law School Scholarship Repository. http://scholarship.law.wm.edu/facpubs/1673.

Finlay, Linda. 2009. Debating Phenomenological Research Methods. *Phenomnenology & Practice* 3, no. 1: 6–25.

Florian, Lani, and John Hegarty. 2004. *ICT and Special Educational Needs: A Tool for Inclusion*. Berkshire: McGraw Hill Education.

Fochtman, Dianne. 2008. Phenomenology in Pediatric Cancer Nursing Research. *Journal of Pediatric Oncology Nursing* 25, no. 4: 185–92. doi:10.1177/1043454208319186.

Freeman, Julie, and Sharna Quirke. 2013. Understanding E-Democracy. *eJournal of eDemocracy & Open Government* 5, no. 2: 141–54.

Freire, A. P., C. M. Russo, and R. P. M. Fortes. 2008. The Perception of Accessibility in Web Development by Academy, Industry and Government: A Survey of the Brazilian Scenario. *The New Review of Hypermedia and Multimedia - Web Accessibility* 14, no. 2: 149–75.

Funilkul, Suree, and Wichian Chutimaskul. 2009. The Framework for Sustainable E-Democracy Development. *Transforming Government: People, Process and Policy* 3, no. 1: 16–31.

Gastil, J. 2000. Is Face-to-Face Deliberation a Luxury or Necessity? *Political Communication* 17: 357–61.

Gibson, Paul, and Victoria Manning. 2013. Political Participation for Everyone: Disabled People's Rights and the Political Process. http://www. internationaldisabilityalliance.org/sites/disalliance.e-presentaciones.net/ files/public/files/NZ NHRI_Political participation for everyone.pdf.

Gibson, R. 2001. Elections Online: Assessing Internet Voting in Light of the Arizona Democratic Primary. *Political Science Quarterly* 116, no. 4: 561–83.

———. 2005. Internet Voting and the European Parliament Elections: Problems and Prospects. In *The European Union and E-Voting: Addressing the European Parliament's Internet Voting Challenge*, edited by A. H. Trechsel and F. Mendez. London and New York: Routledge.

Gisselquist, R. M. 2012. Good Governance as a Concept, and Why This Matters for Development Policy. 2012/30. Helsinki.

Grindle, M.S. 2007. Good Enough Governance Revisited. *Development Policy Review (Special Issue) Developmental States in the New Millennium* 25, no. 5: 533–74.

Groce, Nora, Gayatri Kembhavi, Shelia Wirz, Raymond Lang, Jean-Francois Trani, and Maria Kett. 2011. Poverty and Disability: A Critical Review of the Literature in Low and Middle - Income Countries. 16. https://www.ucl.ac.uk/ lc-ccr/centrepublications/workingpapers/WP16_Poverty_and_Disability_ review.pdf.

Gronke, P., E. Galanes-Rosenbaum, P. A. Miller, and D. Toffey. 2008. Convenience Voting - Annual Review of Political Science. *Political Science* 11: 437–55.

Gronke, P., and P.A. Miller. 2007. Voting by Mail and Turnout: A Replication and Extension. *Annual Meeting of the American Political Science Association* August.

Grönlund, K., and H. Milner. 2006. The Determinants of Political Knowledge in Comparative Perspective. *Scandinavian Political Studies* 29, no. 4: 386–406.

Gutmann, A., and D. Thompson. 1996. *Democracy and Disagreement*. Cambridge, MA: Harvard University Press.

Gwatkin, D.R., S. Rutstein, K. Johnson, E. Suliman, A. Wagstaff, and A. Amouzou. 2007. Socioeconomic Differences in Health, Nutrition, and Population within Developing Countries. 30544. Washington.

Hacker, Kenneth L., and Jan van Dijk. 2000. *Digital Democracy: Issues of Theory and Practice*. Sage Publications Ltd. doi:http://dx.doi.org/10.4135/9781446218891.

Hanna, William John, and Betsy Rogovsky. 1991. Women with Disabilities: Two Handicaps Plus. *Disability, Handicap & Society* 6, no. 1: 49–63.

Hanson, V.L. 2001. Institutional and Web Activities: Web Access for Elderly Citizens. In *WUAUC'01 Proceedings of the 2001 EC/NSF Workshop on Universal Accessibility of Ubiquitous Computing: Providing for the Elderly*. Alcácer do Sal, Portugal.

Haspel, M., and H.G. Knotts. 2005. Location, Location, Location: Precinct Placement and the Costs of Voting. *The Journal of Politics* 67, no. 12: 560–73.

Hersh, Marion, and Michael A. Johnson. 2010. *Assistive Technology for Visually Impaired and Blind People*. Springer Science & Business Media.

Hilgers, Dennis, and Christoph Ihl. 2010. Citizensourcing: Applying the Concept of Open Innovation to the Public Sector. *The International Journal of Public Participation* 4, no. 1: 67–88.

Hong, S., P. Katerattanakul, and S.J. Joo. 2008. Evaluating Government Website Accessibility: A Comparative Study. *International Journal of Information Technology & Decision Making* 7, no. 3: 491–515.

Hull, Daryll, Graham West, and Dubravka Cecez-Kecmanovic. 2010. Two Models of E-Democracy: A Case Study of Government Online Engagement with the Community. In *World Academy of Science, Engineering and Technology Conference, Paris, 2010; UNSW Australian School of Business Research Paper No. 2011-IRRC-01*. https://papers.ssrn.com/sol3/papers.cfm?abstract_id=1782383.

Inglehart, R. 1990. *Culture Shift in Advanced Industrial Societies*. Princeton, NJ: Princeton University Press.

International Telecommunications Union. 2012. Making ICTs Accessible to People with Disabilities. https://www.itu.int/en/wcit-12/Documents/WCIT-background-brief13.pdf.

———. 2013. The ICT Opportunity for a Disability-Inclusive Development Framework: Synthesis Report of the ICT Consultation in Support of the High-Level Meeting on Disability and Development of the Sixty-Eighth Session of the United Nations General Assembly, Geneva. https://www.itu.int/en/action/accessibility/Documents/The ICT Opportunity for a Disability_Inclusive Development Framework.

Internet Society. 2014. Global Internet Report. *Internet Society*. http://www.internetsociety.org/map/global-internet-report/.

Istenic Starcic, Andreja, and Spela Bagon. 2014. ICT-Supported Learning for Inclusion of People with Special Needs: Review of Seven Educational Technology Journals, 1970–2011. *British Journal of Educational Technology* 45, no. 2: 202–30. doi:10.1111/bjet.12086.

Jaeger, P.T. 2006. Assessing Section 508 Compliance on Federal E-Government Web Sites: A Multi-Method, User-Centered Evaluation of Accessibility for Persons with Disabilities. *Government Information Quarterly* 23, no. 2: 169–90.

Jamaica Information Service. 2009. Public Sector Reform in Jamaica. *Jamaica Information Service*. http://jis.gov.jm/public-sector-reform-in-jamaica/.

Jamaica Observer. 2014. End Poverty among Special-Needs Jamaicans. *Jamaica Observer: Health,* September 7. http://www.jamaicaobserver.com/health/ End-poverty-among-special-needs-Jamaicans_17438153.

———. 2016. JLP Presents 10-Point Plan for ICT Sector. http://www.jamaicaobserver. com/news/JLP-presents-10-point-plan-for-ICT-sector_52057.

James, G. 2000. Empowering Bureaucrats. *MC Technology Marketing Intelligence* 20 (12): 62–68.

Johnson, G.B, and S.R. Ryu. 2010. Repudiating or Rewarding Neoliberalism? How Broken Campaign Promises Condition Economic Voting in Latin America. *Latin American Politics and Society* 52, no. 4: 1–24.

Karp, J. A., and S. A. Banducci. 2000. Going Postal: How All-Mail Elections Influence Turnout. *Political Behavior* 22, no. 4: 223–39.

Keane, John. 2009. *The Life and Death of Democracy.* London: Simon & Schuster.

Kelly, C. 2007. Five Main Ways to Use Social Networking in Politics. *New Politics Institute.* http://www.newpolitics.net/sites/ndn-newpol.civicactions.net/files/ NPI_Leverage_Social_Networks.pdf.

Kim, J., and E.J. Kim. 2008. Theorizing Dialogic Deliberation: Everyday Political Talk as Communicative Action and Dialogue. *Communication Theory* 18: 51–70.

Kingston, Richard. 2007. Public Participation in Local Policy Decision-Making: The Role of Web-Based Mapping. *The Carthographic Journal* 44, no. 2: 138–44.

Kousser, T., and M. Mullin. 2007. Does Voting by Mail Increase Participation? Using Matching to Analyze a Natural Experiment. *Political Analysis* 15, no. 4: 428–45.

Kousser, T., M. Mullin, and J. R. Haynes. 2006. *Will Vote-by-Mail Elections Increase Participation? Evidence from California Counties.* Project Sponsored by the John Randolph Haynes and Dora Haynes Foundation.

Koutkias, Vassilis, Nick Kaklanis, Konstantinos Votis, Dimitrios Tzovaras, and Nicos Maglaveras. 2016. An Integrated Semantic Framework Supporting Universal Accessibility to ICT. *Universal Access in the Information Society* 15, no. 1: 49–62. doi:10.1007/s10209-014-0372-1.

Kumar, R., and M. L. Best. 2006. 'Impact and Sustainability of E-Government Services in Developing Countries: Lessons Learned from Tamil Nadu, India.' *The Information Society* 22, no. 1: 1–12.

Kuzma, J. M. 2009. Regulatory Compliance and Web Accessibility of UK Parliament Sites. *Journal of Information Law & Technology (JILT)* 2: 1–15. <http:// go.warwick.ac.uk/jilt/2009_2/kuzma>.

Lau, E. 2003. Challenges for E-Government Development. In *5th Global Forum on Reinventing Government.* Mexico City.

Lawson, Anna. 2014. Monitoring Political Participation Rights of Blind and Partially-Sighted People in Europe: An Analysis of the European Blind Union CRPD Database. http://www.euroblind.org/media/ebu-media/ebu-report-art29. pdf.

Layne, Karen, and Jungwoo Lee. 2001. Developing Fully Functional E-Government: A Four-Stage Model. *Government Information Quarterly* 18, no. 2: 122–36.

Lee, Jungwoo. 2010. 10 Year Retrospect on Stage Models of E-Government: A Qualitative Meta-Synthesis. *Government Information Quarterly* 27, no. 3: 220–30.

Leftwich, A. 1993. Governance, Democracy and Development in the Third World. *Third World Quarterly* 14: 605–24.

Lemmetty, Sami. 1999. Review of Speech Synthesis Technology. Helsinki University of Technology. research.spa.aalto.fi/publications/theses/lemmetty_mst/thesis.pdf.

LeVasseur, J. J. 2003. The Problem of Bracketing in Phenomenology. *Qualitative Health Research* 13, no. 3: 408–20.

Lindner, R., and U. Riehm. 2008. Electronic Petitions and the Relationship between Institutional Contexts, Technology and Political Participation. In *Edem2008. International Conference on Electronic Democracy (Proceedings) Linz, Österreichische Computer Gesellschaft*, edited by P. Parycek and A. Prosser.

———. 2009. Electronic Petitions and Institutional Modernization. *eJournal of eDemocracy and Open Government* 1, no. 1: 1–11.

Linton, Lantonya. 2013. E-Government Initiative Moving Ahead. *Jamaica Information Service.* http://jis.gov.jm/e-government-initiative-moving-ahead/.

Lopez, K. A., and D. G. Willis. 2004. Descriptive versus Interpretive Phenomenology: Their Contribution to Nursing Knowledge. *Qualitative Health Research* 14, no. 5: 726–35.

Lord, J. E., M. A. Stein, and J. Fiala-Butora. 2014. Facilitating an Equal Right to Vote for Persons with Disabilities. *Journal of Human Rights Practice* 6, no. 5: 115–39.

Luechinger, S., M. Rosinger, and A. Stutzer. 2007. The Impact of Postal Voting on Participation: Evidence for Switzerland. *Swiss Political Science Review* 13, no. 2: 67–202.

Macintosh, Ann, and Angus Whyte. 2006. Evaluating How E- Participation Changes Local Democracy. Paper Presented at the eGovernment Workshop, Brunel University. West London: eGovernment Workshop, Brunel University.

Macnamara, Jim. 2012. Democracy 2.0 Can Social Media Engage Youth and Disengaged Citizens in the Public Sphere? *Australian Journal of Communication* 39, no. 3: 65–86.

Magleby, D.B. 1987. Participation in Mail Ballot Elections. *The Western Political Quarterly* 40, no. 1: 79–91.

Mankoff, J., H. Fait, and T. Tran. 2005. Is Your Web Page Accessible? A Comparative Study of Methods for Assessing Web Page Accessibility for the Blind. In *CHI '05 Proceedings of the SIGCHI Conference on Human Factors in Computing Systems*. Portland, Oregon.

Mansbridge, J. 1993. Governance, Democracy and Development in the Third World. *Third World Quarterly* 14: 605–24.

Memoli, V. 2011. How Does Political Knowledge Shape Support for Democracy? Some Research Based on the Italian Case. *Bulletin of Italian Politics* 3, no. 1: 79–102.

Milner, H. 2008. The Informed Political Participation of Young Canadians and Americans. 60. CIRCLE Working Paper. Montreal. http://www.civicyouth.org/PopUps/WorkingPapers/WP60Milner.pdf.

Ministry of Justice. 2015. Ministry of Justice. http://www.moj.gov.jm.

Mofleh, S., M. Wanous, and P. Strachan. 2008. The Gap between Citizens and E-Government Projects: The Case for Jordan. *Electronic Government, an International Journal* 5, no. 3: 275–87.

Moon, D. 1990. What You Use Depends on What You Have: Information Effects on the Determinants of Electoral Choice. *American Politics Quarterly* 18: 3–24.

Mosca, Lorenzo, and Daria Santucci. 2009. Petitioning Online: The Role of E-Petitions in Web Campaigning. In *Political Campaigning on the Web*, edited by Sigrid Baringhorst, Veronika Kneip, and Johanna Niesyto, 121–46. Bielefeld: Transcript.

Mossberger, Karen, Caroline J. Tolbert, and Ramona S. McNeal. 2008. *Digital Citizenship: The Internet, Society, and Participation*. Cambridge, MA: MIT Press.

Moyes, Adrian. 1981. *One in Ten. Disability and the Very Poor*. Oxford: Oxfam GB.

National Committee on Political Tribalism. 1997. Report of the National Committee on Political Tribalism. Kingston, Jamaica.

National Federation of the Blind. 2006. National Federation of the Blind Unveils World's First Handheld Electronic Reader. https://nfb.org/node/1268.

Nchise, Abinwi C. 2012. The Trend of E-Democracy Research: Summary Evidence and Implications. In *Proceedings of the 13th Annual International Conference on Digital Government Research*, 165–72. New York. doi:10.1145/2307729.2307756.

Neblo, Michael. 2005. Thinking through Democracy: Between the Theory and Practice of Deliberative Politics. *Acta Politica* 40, no. 2: 169–81. doi:10.1057/palgrave.ap.5500102.

Nicholson, S.P., A. Pantoja, and G.M. Segura. 2006. Political Knowledge and Issue Voting among the Latino Electorate. *Political Research Quarterly* 59, no. 2: 259–71.

Norris, Donald F. 2010. E-Government...Not E-Governance...Not E-Democracy Not Now!: Not Ever? In *ICEGOV '10 Proceedings of the 4th International Conference on Theory and Practice of Electronic Governance*, 339–46. New York. doi:10.1145/1930321.1930391.

Norris, P. 2004. E-Voting as the Magic Ballot for European Parlimentary Elections? Evaluating E-Voting in the Light Ofexperiments in UK Local Elections. In *The European Union and E-Voting: Addressing the European Parliament's Internet Voting Challenge*, 60–90. London: Routledge.

Nosek, M. A., C. Howland, D. H. Rintala, M. E. Young, and G. F. Chanpong. 2001. National Study of Women with Physical Disabilities: Final Report. *Sexuality and Disability* 19, no. 1: 5–40.

OECD. 2001. *Citizens as Partners: OECD Handbook on Information, Consultation and Public Participation in Policy-Making*. Paris: OECD Publications.

Olphert, W., and L. Damodaran. 2007. Citizen Participation and Engagement in the Design of E-Government Services: The Missing Link in Effective ICT Design and Delivery. *Journal of the Association for Information Systems* 8, no. 9: 27.

Oostveen, A-M., and P. Van den Besselaar. 2004. Internet Voting Technologies and Civic Participation: The Users' Perspective. *Javnost* 11, no. 1: 61–78.

Oostveen, Anne-Marie, and Peter van den Besselaar. 2004a. From Small Scale to Large Scale User Participation: A Case Study of Participatory Design in E-Government Systems. In *Proceedings of the Eighth Conference on Participatory Design: Artful Integration: Interweaving Media, Materials and Practices - Volume 1*, 173–82. New York: ACM.

———. 2004b. Internet Voting Technologies and Civic Participation: The Users' Perspective. *Javnost* 11, no. 1: 61–78.

Organization of American States. 1995. EDUCATION: Investment in Education. Retrieved February 1, 2017 from http://www.summit-americas.org/sisca/ed_inv.html

Orum, A.M., and J.G. Dale. 2008. *Introduction to Political Sociology: Power and Participation in the Modern World*. USA: Oxford University Press.

Oxley, Zoe M. 2012. More Sources, Better Informed Public? New Media and Political Knowledge. In *iPolitics: Citizens, Elections, and Governing in the New Media Era*, edited by Richard L. Fox and Jennifer M. Ramos. New York: Cambridge University Press.

Palanisamy, R., and B. Mukerji. 2012. *Security and Privacy Issues in E-Government*. Canada: IGI Global.

Palmer, J. 2002. Designing for Web Site Usability. *Computer* 35, no. 7: 102–3.

Palvia, S.C.J., and S. S. Sharma. 2007. E-Government and E-Governance: Definitions/domain Framework and Status around the World. In *International Conference on E-Governance*, 1–12.

Panagiotopoulos, Panagiotis (Panos), and Mutaz M. Al-Debei. 2010. Engaging with Citizens Online: Understanding the Role of ePetitioning in Local Government Democracy. In *Paper Presented at: Internet, Politics, Policy 2010: An Impact Assessment St Anne's College, University of Oxford*.

Paris, M. 2006. Website Accessibility: A Survey of Local E-Government Websites and Legislation in Northern Ireland. *Universal Access in the Information Society* 4, no. 4: 292–99.

Pedwell, Carolyn, and Diane Perrons. 2007. The Politics of Democratic Governance Organising for Social Inclusion and Gender Equity. http://win.amarc.org/documents/The PoliticsofGovernance.pdf.

Peet, R., and E. Hartwick. 2015. *Theories of Development: Contentions, Arguments, Alternatives*. Guilford Publications.

Peters, G. L. 2003. *The Prospects of I-Voting in America*. Blacksburg: Virginia Polytechnic Institute and State University.

PIOJ. 2009. Vision 2030 Jamaica: National Development Plan. *Planning Institute of Jamaica*. http://www.vision2030.gov.jm./SectoPlans.aspx.

Price, V., and J. Zaller. 1993. Who Gets the News? Alternative Measures of News Reception and Their Implications for Research. *Political Opinion Quarterly* 57, no. 2: 133–64.

Prior, M. 2007. *Post-Broadcast Democracy: How Media Choice Increases Inequality in Political Involvement and Polarizes Elections*. Cambridge University Press.

Rabaiah, A., and E. Vandijck. 2009. A Strategic Framework of E-Government: Generic and Best Practice. *Electronic Journal of E-Government* 7, no. 3: 241–58.

Raja, Deepti Samant. 2016. Bridging the Disability Divide through Digital Technologies. pubdocs.worldbank.org/pubdocs/publicdoc/2016/4/1234814 61249337484.

Raymond, Duane. 2010. eCampaigning Models: Email-to-Action. *FairSay*. http://fairsay.com/blog/2010/ecampaigning-models-email-to-action.

Reiners, Gina M. 2012. Understanding the Differences between Husserl's (Descriptive) and Heideggers (Interpretive) Phenomenological Research. *J Nurs Care 1:119* 1 (5). doi:10.4172/2167-1168.1000119.

Reith, Lorna. 1994. Exploring the Links between Poverty and Disability – the Extra Costs of Disability. In *Disability, Exclusion & Poverty: A Policy Conference.* Combat Poverty Agency, the Forum of People with Disabilities and the National Rehabilitation Board.

Resnick, D., and R. Birner. 2006. Does Good Governance Contribute to Pro-Poor Growth?: A Review of the Evidence from Cross-Country Studies. Discussion Paper No. 30. Washington, DC: DSDG, International Food Policy Research Institute.

Reynal-Querol, M. 2005. Does democracy preempt civil wars? *European Journal of Political Economy,* 21 (2), 445–65.

Riley, C. G. 2003. The Changing Role of the Citizen in the E-Governance & E-Democracy Equation. Commonwealth Centre for e-Governance.

Riley, T.B. 2003. E-Government Vs. E-Governance: Examining the Differences in a Changing Public Sector Climate. *International Tracking Survey Reports.*

Robinson, James A. 2006. Economic Development and Democracy. *Annu. Rev. Polit. Sci* 9: 503–27.

Rodrik, Dani, and Romain Wacziarg. 2005. Do Democratic Transtions Produce Bad Economic Outcome? *The Americian Economic Review* 95, no. 2: 50–55.

Rose, Damon. 2013. Blind Drivers at the Steering Wheel. *BBC News.* April. www.bbc.com/news/magazine-21720318.

Sachs, Jeffrey D. 2005. *United Nations Millennium Project Investing in Development: A Practical Plan to Achieve the Millennium Development Goals Report to the UN Secretary General.* New York: United Nations Development Programme (UNDP).

Sæbø, Øystein, Jeremy Rose, and Leif Skiftenes Flak. 2008. The Shape of eParticipation: Characterizing an Emerging Research Area. *Government Information Quarterly* 25, no. 3: 400–428.

Sanders, Carolyn. 2003. Application of Colaizzi's Method: Interpretation of an Auditable Decision Trail by a Novice Researcher. *Contemporary Nurse Journal* 14, no. 3: 292–302.

Sandlin, Robert E. 2000. *Textbook of Hearing Aid Amplification.* Cengage Learning.

Santucci, Daria. 2007. Studying E-Petitions: State of the Art and Challenges. In *ESF-LiU Conference Electronic Democracy: Achievements and Challenges – Vadstena, Sweden – 21-25 November 2007.*

Scherer, Marcia J, and Rob Glueckauf. 2005. Assessing the Benefits of Assistive Technologies for Activities and Participation. *Rehabiliation Psychology* 50, no. 2: 132–41. doi:10.1037/0090-5550.50.2.132.

Schraufnagel, S., and B. Sgouraki. 2005. Voter Turnout in Central and South America. *The Latin Americanist* 49, no. 2: 39–69.

Schur, Lisa, Meera Adya, and Douglas Kruse. 2013. Disability, Voter Turnout, and Voting Difficulties in the 2012 Elections. http://smlr.rutgers.edu/disability-and-voting-survey-report-2012-elections.

Seifert, Jeffrey W., and G. Matthew Bonham. 2003. The Transformative Potential of E-Government in Transitional Democracies. *Public Management. Electronic Journal*, no. 2:22.

Seymour-Ford, Jan. 2009. History of the Perkins Brailler. *Perkins School for the Blind.* www.perkins.org/assets/downloads/research/history-of-brailler-11.

Sharma, Kriti. 2014. Treated Worse than Animals : Abuses against Women and Girls with Psychosocial or Intellectual Disabilities in Institutions in India. http://www.asksource.info/RESOURCES/TREATED-WORSE-ANIMALS-ABUSES-AGAINST-WOMEN-AND-GIRLS-PSYCHOSOCIAL-OR-INTELLECTUAL.

Shi, Y. 2006. E-Government Web Site Accessibility in Australia and China: A Longitudinal Study. *Social Science Computer Review* 24, no. 3: 378–85.

Shosha, G.A. 2012. Employment of Colaizzi's Strategy in Descriptive Phenomenology: A Reflection of a Researcher. *European Scientific Journal* 8 (27).

Simpson, J. 2009. Inclusive Information and Communication Technologies for People with Disabilities. *Disability Studies Quarterly* 29, no. 1.

Sives, Amanda. 2002. Changing Patrons, from Politician to Drug Don: Clientelism in Downtown Kingston, Jamaica. *Latin American Perspectives* 29, no. 5: 66–89.

Southwell, P.L., and J.I. Burchett. 2000. The Effect of All-Mail Elections on Voter Turnout. *American Politics Research* 28, no. 1: 72–79.

Speziale, Helen J. Streubert, and Dona Rinaldi Carpenter. 2007. *Qualitative Research in Nursing: Advancing the Humanistic Imperative.* 4th ed. Philadelphia: Lippincott Williams & Wilkins.

Stanyer, James. 2005. Political Parties, the Internet and the 2005 General Election: From Web Presence to E-Campaigning? *Journal of Marketing Management* 21, no. 9–10: 1049–65.

Statistics New Zealand. 2006. 2006 Household Disability Survey. *2006 Disability Survey.* http://www.stats.govt.nz/browse_for_stats/health/disabilities/DisabilitySurvey2006_HOTP06/Technical Notes.aspx.

———. 2013. Disability Survey 2013. http://www.stats.govt.nz/browse_for_stats/health/disabilities/DisabilitySurvey_HOTP2013.aspx.

Stein, Robert M. 1998. Introduction: Early Voting. *The Public Opinion Quarterly* 62, no. 1: 57–69. www.jstor.org/.

Stienstra, Deborah, and Lindsey Troschuk. 2005. Engaging Citizens with Disabilities in E-Democracy. *Disability Studies Quarterly* 25, no. 2. www.dsq-sds.org.

Stone, Carl. 1980. *Democracy and Clientelism in Jamaica.* New Brunswick, USA: Transaction Books.

Stratford, J. S., and J. Stratford. 2001. Computerized and Networked Government Information. *Journal of Government Information* 28, no. 3: 297–301.

Taylor-Smith, E., and R. Lindner. 2009. Using Social Networking Tools to Promote eParticipation Initiatives. In *Proceedings of EDEM 2009 - Conference on Electronic Democracy, September 7-8, 2009, Vienna*, edited by A. Prosser and P. Parycek, 115–21. Vienna: Austrian Computer Society.

The Cabinet Office. 2002. Government at Your Service: Public Sector Modernisation Vision and Strategy 2002-2012. *Ministry Paper 56/02.* http://www.cabinet.gov.jm/files/govatyourservice.pdf.

The World Bank. 2008. *Social Inclusion through ICT for Tunisian Disabled.* Social inclusion through ICT for Tunisian disabled.

United Nations. 2005. World Programme of Action Concerning Disabled Persons. *United Nations Enable.* http://www.un.org/disabilities/default.asp?id=23.

———. 2008. *Participatory Governance and the Millennium Development Goals (MDGs).* New York.

———. 2011. *Disability and the Millennium Development Goals: A Review of the MDG Process and Strategies for Inclusion of Disability Issues in Millennium Development Goal Efforts.* New York: United Nations Publications.

———. 2014. *United Nations E-Government Survey 2014.* New York.

United Nations Department of Economic and Social Affairs. 2016. *United Nations E-Government Survey 2016: E-Government in Support of Sustainable Development.* New York: United Nations.

Valenzuela, Sebastian, Namsu Park, and Kerk F Kee. 2009. Is There Social Capital in a Social Network Site?: Facebook Use and College Students' Life Satisfaction, Trust and Participation. *Computer-Mediated Communication* 14, no. 4: 875–901. doi:10.1111/j.1083-6101.2009.01474.x.

van Manen, Max. 1990. *Researching Lived Experience: Human Science for an Action Sensitive Pedagogy.* Ontario, Canada: The Althouse Press.

van Reijswoud, Victor. 2009. Appropriate ICT as a Tool to Increase Effectiveness in ICT4D: Theoretical Considerations and Illustrating Cases. *The Electronic Journal of Information Systems in Developing Countries* 38.

Vanderheiden, Gregg C. 1998. Universal Design and Assistive Technology in Communication Technologies: Alternatives or Complements? *Assistive Technology* 10, no. 1: 29–36. doi:10.1080/10400435.1998.10131958.

Varela, K. 2010. I Don't Trust Them: Latino Perceptions of Discrimination and Identity, and What This Means for Latino Trust in the Government. College of Arts & Sciences, Illinois State University.

Vergeer, Maurice, Liesbeth Hermans, and Steven Sams. 2013. Online Social Networks and Micro-Blogging in Political Campaigning The Exploration of a New Campaign Tool and a New Campaign Style. *Party Politics* 19, no. 3: 477–501.

Waller, L.G. 2013. Enhancing Political Participation in Jamaica. *SAGE Open* 3, no. 2.

Waller, L.G., and A. Genius. 2015. Barriers to Transforming Government in Jamaica: Challenges to Implementing Initiatives to Enhance the Efficiency, Effectiveness and Service Delivery of Government through ICTs (E-Government). *Transforming Government: People, Process and Polic* 9, no. 4: 480–97.

Waller, L. 2016. There is an App for That Too: Citizen-centric Approach to Combating Corruption in the Digital Age through the use of ICTs. In *Political Scandal, Corruption and Legitimacy in the Age of Social Media,* ed. K. Demirhan and D. Çakir-Demirhan. Hershey, PA: IGI Global

Walsh, Barry. 2011. E-Justice Projects – Distinguishing Myths from Realities. Mexico City. http://www.iijusticia.org/docs/Barry.pdf.

Wandhoefer, Timo, Mark Thamm, and Somya Joshi. 2011. Politician 2.0: Information Behavior and Dissemination on Social Networking Sites - Gaps and Best-Practices. *eJournal of eDemocracy & Open Government* 3, no. 2: 207–14.

Wantchekon, L. 2003. Clientelism and Voting Behavior: Evidence from a Field Experiment in Benin. *World Politics* 55, no. 3: 399–422.

Warkentin, Merrill, David Gefen, Paul A. Pavlou, and Gregory M. Rose. 2002. Encouraging Citizen Adoption of E-Government by Building Trust. *Electronic Markets* 12, no. 3: 157–62.

Washington Univesrsity School of Medicine. 2009. Timeline of Hearing Devices and Early Deaf Education. *Deafness in Disguise.* beckerexhibits.wustl.edu/did/timeline/index.htm.

Watkins, A. 2014. *Model Policy for Inclusive ICTs in Education for Persons with Disabilities.* Geneva: UNESCO, European Agency for Special Needs and Inclusive Education, G3ict.

Weatherford, M.S. 1989. Political Economy and Political Legitimacy: The Link between Economic Policy and Political Trust. In *Economic Decline and Political Change: Canada, Great Britain, and the United States,* edited by H.D. Clarke, M.C. Stewart, and G. Zuk, 225–48. Pittsburgh, PA: University of Pittsburgh Press.

WHO. 2011. World Report on Disability. World Health Organization. http://www.who.int/disabilities/world_report/2011/report.pdf.

———. 2012. Disabilities. *World Health Organization: Health Topics.* http://www.who.int/topics/disabilities/en/.

Wildermuth, J. 2006. SANTA ROSA / Disabled Try out Voting Machines for Accessibility / Counties Scramble to Have Equipment in Place for June 6 Election. *SFGATE.* SANTA ROSA / Disabled try out voting machines for accessibility / Counties scramble to have equipment in place for June 6 election.

Williams, Andrew Paul, and Evan Serge. 2014. Evaluating Candidate E-Mail Messages in the 2008 US Presidential Campaign. In *Techno Politics in Presidential Campaigning: New Voices, New Technologies, and New Voters,* edited by John Hendricks and Lynda Lee Kaid. New York: Routledge.

Willis, Sarah. 2015. New Tech Is Changing Lives for the Visually Impaired. *Tech.Co.* tech.co/new-tech-changing-life-visually-impaired-2015-01.

Wojnar, Danuta M, and Kristen M Swanson. 2007. Phenomenology an Exploration. *Journal of Holistic Nursing* 25, no. 3: 172–80. doi:10.1177/0898010106295172.

Wong, Wilson, and Eric Welch. 2004. Does E-Government Promote Accountability? A Comparative Analysis of Website Openness and Government Accountability. *Governance: An International Journal of Policy, Administration, and Institutions* 17, no. 2: 275–97.

World Bank. 2006. *World Development Report 2007: Development and the Next Generation.* Washington, DC.

———. 2011. E-Security. http://web.worldbank.org/WBSITE/EXTERNAL/TOPICS/EXTINFORMATIONANDCOMMUNICATIONANDTECHNOLOGIES/EXTEDEVELOPMENT/0,,contentMDK:21264365~menuPK:4053985~pagePK:210058~piPK:210062~theSitePK:559460,00.html.

———. 2016. Overview. http://www.worldbank.org/en/topic/disability/overview.

WWDA. 2012. An Overview of the Status of Women With Disabilities in Australia. *Women with Disabilities Australia.* http://wwda.org.au/about/snapshot/.

Young, Iris Marion. 2002. *Inclusion and Democracy.* Oxford: Oxford University Press.

Index

www.ingramcontent.com/pod-product-compliance
Lightning Source LLC
La Vergne TN
LVHW022350060326
832902LV00022B/4348